QUES

AMERICAN LITERATURE
Volume 2

Prepared by
Heidi LM Jacobs
University of Windsor

New York Boston San Francisco
London Toronto Sydney Tokyo Singapore Madrid
Mexico City Munich Paris Cape Town Hong Kong Montreal

Jacobs, *Questions to accompany Cain, American Literature, Volume 2*

Copyright ©2004 Pearson Education, Inc.

All rights reserved. Printed in the United States of America. Instructors may reproduce portions of this book for classroom use only. All other reproductions are strictly prohibited without prior permission of the publisher, except in the case of brief quotations embodied in critical articles and reviews.

ISBN: 0-321-28035-0

1 2 3 4 5 6 7 8 9 10–CRW–06 05 04

CONTENTS *by Author*

Part I: Literature at the End of the Nineteenth Century   1
Samuel L. Clemens   3
Bret Harte   3
W. D. Howells   4
Sidney Lanier   4
Ambrose Bierce   4
Henry James   5
Joel Chandler Harris   5
Sarah Orne Jewett   6
Emma Lazarus   7
Kate Chopin   7
Mary Wilkins Freeman   7
Booker T. Washington   7
Charles Chesnutt   8
Hamlin Garland   8
Charlotte Perkins Gilman   9
Edith Wharton   9
W. E. B. Du Bois   10
Stephen Crane   10
Theodore Dreiser   11
Jack London   11

Part II: Modern American Literature   13
Edgar Lee Masters   15
Edwin Arlington Robinson   15
Paul Laurence Dunbar   16
Willa Cather   17
Gertrude Stein   17
Amy Lowell   17
Robert Frost   19
Sherwood Anderson   24
Carl Sandburg   24
Wallace Stevens   24
Susan Glaspell   27
William Carlos Williams   28
Ezra Pound   31
H.D. (Hilda Doolittle)   32
Robinson Jeffers   33
Marianne Moore   34

T.S. Eliot	35
Eugene O'Neill	37
John Crowe Ransom	37
Claude McKay	38
Katherine Anne Porter	39
Zora Neale Hurston	39
Archibald MacLeish	39
Edna St. Vincent Millay	40
E.E. Cummings	42
James Thurber	44
Jean Toomer	45
F. Scott Fitzgerald	45
Louise Bogan	46
William Faulkner	47
Ernest Hemingway	48
Hart Crane	48
Sterling A. Brown	49
Langston Hughes	50
Countee Cullen	54
Richard Wright	55
Muriel Rukeyser	55

Part III: American Prose Since 1945 — 57

Eudora Welty	59
Tennessee Williams	59
John Cheever	60
Bernard Malamud	60
Ralph Ellison	61
Grace Paley	61
James Baldwin	62
Flannery O'Connor	62
Martin Luther King, Jr.	62
Toni Morrison	63
John Updike	63
Philip Roth	64
Amiri Baraka	64
Joyce Carol Oates	65
Raymond Carver	65
Toni Cade Bambara	65
Terrance McNally	66
Bobbie Ann Mason	66
Anne Tyler	67

Alice Walker	67
Tobias Wolff	67
Tim O'Brien	68
Leslie Marmon Silko	68
Amy Tan	69
Alice Elliott Dark	69
Louise Erdrich	69
David Henry Hwang	70
David Leavitt	70
Suzan-Lori Parks	71

Part IV: American Poetry Since 1945 — 73

Robert Penn Warren	75
George Oppen	76
Theodore Roethke	77
Charles Olson	79
Elizabeth Bishop	79
Robert Hayden	81
Dudley Randall	82
William Stafford	82
Randall Jarrell	83
John Berryman	83
Robert Lowell	85
Gwendolyn Brooks	86
Lawrence Ferlinghetti	87
Robert Duncan	87
Richard Wilbur	88
James Dickey	89
Mitsuye Yamada	90
Denise Levertov	90
A.R. Ammons	92
James Merrill	92
Robert Creeley	92
Allen Ginsberg	94
Frank O'Hara	95
Galway Kinnell	96
John Ashbery	96
W.S. Merwin	97
James Wright	98
Philip Levine	99
Anne Sexton	99
Adrienne Rich	100

Gary Snyder	101
Sylvia Plath	101
Linda Pastan	103
Amiri Baraka	103
Mary Oliver	103
Marge Piercy	105
Lucille Clifton	105
Michael S. Harper	105
Paula Gunn Allen	106
Gloria Anzaldúa	107
Joseph Bruchac III	107
Sharon Olds	107
Tess Gallagher	108
Nikki Giovanni	108
Louise Glück	109
Yusef Komunyakaa	110
Joy Harjo	111
Jimmy Santiago Baca	112
Rita Dove	112
Judith Ortiz Cofer	114
Alberto Ríos	114
David Mura	114
Laureen Mar	115
Lorna Dee Cervantes	116
Aurora Levins Morales	116
Cathy Song	116
Li-Young Lee	117
Martin Espada	118
Sherman Alexie	119

PART I

American Literature at the End of the Nineteenth Century

Samuel L. Clemens,
The Notorious Jumping Frog of Calaveras County

1. Examine Twain's structure of using two different voices. Why does he use the two voices? What effect do they have?
2. How and where does he create humor? How does Twain use humor in this story?
3. Connect this story with the tradition of the short story. How does it fit in with that tradition?

Samuel L. Clemens,
Fenimore Cooper's Literary Offences

1. What is Clemens' tone in this piece? Is he serious or satiric? Support your answer with specifics from the text.
2. What is the basis of this critique of Cooper? Is it valid? What is the narrator suggesting are Cooper's "greatest offences"? What is he suggesting about literary taste and literary criticism?
3. In the final paragraphs, the narrator discusses what art is. According to the narrator, what is art? Do you agree with the narrator?
4. What is the significance of the final line? How does this line relate to the rest of this piece?

Bret Harte,
The Outcasts of Poker Flat

1. Explain the significance of the statement that Oakhurst was "at once the strongest and yet the weakest of the outcasts of Poker Flats."
2. Connect Harte's story with the tradition of local color writing.
3. Discuss the concepts of chance, luck, and games in relation to one of the story's characters.

W. D. Howells,
Editha

1. Consider the significance of this story's historical setting. What does the setting add to the story and its themes?
2. Select two characters and examine their perspectives on war. How are they similar? Different? Why are they similar or different? With whom do you agree? Why?
3. Do a character sketch of Editha. What are her motivations? Does she change? What are her priorities and values? How does Howells convey Editha's character?
4. Explicate the final five paragraphs and explain their significance to the story. What does this ending contribute to the story?

Sidney Lanier,
The Dying Words of Stonewall Jackson

1. Who is Stonewall Jackson? Why might he be the subject of a poem? What is the narrator's tone toward Jackson? How is this tone created?
2. Analyze this poem in the context of the Civil War. Why might the date September 1865 be significant to understanding this poem?
3. Examine Lanier's use of poetic devices such as diction and figurative language. What kind of diction is used? What kind of imagery? What is the overall effect of these devices on the poem?

Ambrose Bierce,
Chickamauga

1. Consider Bierce's style in this story. How would you characterize his style? What are the dominant features of his style and how are these features used for effect?
2. Who (or what) are the men that the boy sees? How are they described? Why are they described in this way?

3. Why might Bierce have chosen to tell this story from this point of view? What is he able to do with this point of view that he would be otherwise unable to do with other points of view?
4. Examine Bierce's depiction of this setting. What is he suggesting through this depiction of this specific time and place in the U.S.?

Henry James,
The Pupil

1. Describe James's treatment of the Moreen family. What does Pemberton notice about them? Why are they of interest to him? What is the nature of the relationship that develops between him and the family?
2. Describe the relationship between Morgan and Pemberton. Upon what is this relationship founded? How does this relationship change? Do Morgan and Pemberton view the relationship differently?
3. Address the recurrent critique of James's writing style that the editor cites: "nothing happens." Address the editor's comment that "for James, 'what happens' is not primarily a series of actions or events but, rather, the complicated movement of consciousness, of thought and feeling." How does this statement apply to this story?
4. Analyze the significance of the story's denouement. Is this an appropriate closure for this story, these characters, and the relationship between the characters?

Joel Chandler Harris,
The Tar-Baby

1. Examine the character of Uncle Remus. How is he depicted? What kind of character is he?
2. What is the effect of Harris' use of dialogue? Why might Harris have chosen to convey this story through dialogue?
3. What is the narrative function of the Tar Baby? What role does it play in the story?

Joel Chandler Harris,
Mr. Rabbit Grossly Deceives Mr. Fox

1. Examine the framing device Harris uses in this story. What function does it have in the story? What does it reveal about the context of the storytelling?
2. What does Harris's use of dialect contribute to the story? What effect does this dialect have on your reading of this story?
3. How might our reading of this story be different from that of this story's original readers? What has changed?

Sarah Orne Jewett,
A White Heron

1. Connect Jewett's story with the local color tradition. What is this tradition and how does this story embody it?
2. Explain the significance of the White Heron from 2 of the characters' perspectives. What does the heron represent and what does the character's reaction to the heron say about the character?
3. Discuss Jewett's depiction of nature and the natural world. How is it described and why is the natural world important to this story?

Emma Lazarus,
The New Colossus

1. This poem has a specific symbolic significance for the United States. Where have you heard this poem before and why is this poem significant for the United States?
2. Who is the woman described and how is she depicted? Why is she depicted in this way?
3. Explain the significance of the material in quotation marks. Why does the woman say this? What is the significance of the imagery in her statement?

Kate Chopin,
The Storm.

1. Explain Chopin's use of the storm. What is its function in the story? How is this setting important or symbolic?
2. Discuss Chopin's use of imagery and diction to convey the theme of marriage and love.
3. Explain the significance of the statement, "so the storm passed and everyone was happy."
4. Do a close reading of Chopin's descriptions of marriages and relationships. What might she be suggesting about the relationships between men and women?

Mary Wilkins Freeman,
The Revolt of "Mother"

1. Consider Freeman's treatment of gender in this story. How are gender issues addressed?
2. Houses and domestic work are central to this story. What is Freeman suggesting about domesticity and domestic life in this story?
3. What is the nature of the "revolt" in this story? Why does Freeman call it a revolt? What is suggested by this word? How does Sarah Penn revolt?
4. Why does the narrator say the minister could "expound the intricacies of every character study in the Scriptures . . . but Sarah Penn was beyond him."

Booker T. Washington,
from Up From Slavery

1. Washington says, "the thing that was uppermost in my mind was the desire to say something that would cement the friendship of the races and bring about hearty cooperation between them." Do you think his speech would have achieved his desire? Do a close reading of this piece and describe why or why not.

2. Analyze this speech as a piece of persuasive rhetoric. Is it a persuasive speech regarding the race situation? What specific elements of this speech do you find the most persuasive?
3. What does Washington mean by "the opportunity to earn a dollar in a factory just now is worth infinitely more than the opportunity to spend a dollar in an opera house." Do you think his audience would have agreed or disagreed with this statement? Why or why not?
4. Washington mentions many names and makes numerous allusions. What effect might these elements have on an audience?

Charles Chesnutt,
The Sheriff's Children

1. Consider the significance of the specific setting of this story (place, time, social and historical context). Why is this setting significant for the story and the themes it addresses?
2. Examine Chesnutt's depiction of the sheriff. What do we know about him? How is he characterized? What does this story reveal about him? What does the sheriff learn about himself?
3. Explore this story as a commentary on race and racism. What issues does it address? What does it suggest about race?
4. Do a character sketch of the prisoner. What are his motivations? What function does he play in this story? How does Chesnutt describe him? What is significant about Chesnutt's depiction of him?

Hamlin Garland,
Under the Lion's Paw

1. Garland was actively engaged in social reform movements. Examine this story in the context of social reform. What reform agendas might this story be advancing? Is this story an effective form of social reform? Why? Why not? What issues does it raise?
2. Explain Stephen Council's and Mrs. Council's role in the story. How are they described? What issues do they raise or convey? How are they related to the story's dominant themes?

3. Do a character sketch of Jim Butler. What are his motivations? What is the narrator's tone toward him? What issues does Garland raise through this character?
4. Describe Garland's depiction of the Haskins family and their relationship with the physical setting and social context. What issues does their story raise about human nature?

Charlotte Perkins Gilman,
The Yellow Wall-Paper

1. Explain how Gilman uses narrative voice. How is the narrator's voice used to convey themes or ideas? How does the first person voice change and to what effect?
2. Describe Gilman's symbolic use of the yellow wallpaper. What is it symbolic of and how does it evolve as a symbol?
3. Choose one minor character and show how he or she connects with the story's themes.
4. Some critics suggest that "The Yellow Wall-Paper" is a form of social critique. What is Gilman critiquing? Is this story an effective mode of social critique?

Edith Wharton,
The Other Two

1. Examine Alice's marriages. What do they reveal about her? About the assumptions regarding marriage? What do the marriages reveal about the three men? Do the men view her marriages differently than Alice does?
2. Select one of the husbands and provide a character sketch of him. How is his character conveyed by Wharton? What does Wharton's character of him reveal? What does he reveal about himself? What do others reveal about him? What is his thematic role in the story?
3. Analyze the thematic significance of the line, "With grim irony, Waythorn compared himself to a member of a syndicate." What does this statement reveal about him, his social context, Alice, and/or marriage?

4. Can this story be read as a form of social commentary or critique? What social issues are raised? What might Wharton be suggesting in this story?

W. E. B. Du Bois, from **The Souls of Black Folk: of Booker T. Washington and Others**

1. Du Bois writes, "Honest and earnest criticism . . . .. is the soul of American democracy and the safeguard of modern society." What is the nature of Du Bois' critique of Booker T. Washington? What points does he make? How is this piece related to the "soul of American democracy"?
2. Examine the number, nature, and range of the footnotes included in this piece. What do these allusions and references contribute to your understanding of this piece, Du Bois' authority as a writer and thinker, and the overall effectiveness and persuasiveness of this piece?
3. Compare the argument in this piece with Booker T. Washington's "Up From Slavery." Who do you think presents the most effective argument about race in America? Is one more effective than the other?
4. Du Bois begins this section with a quotation from Byron and music from Black spirituals. What effect do these two elements have on the piece? What assumptions or questions do they raise?

Stephen Crane, **An Episode of War**

1. Describe Crane's style. Is this an effective style for the depiction of a war story? Explain why or why not?
2. Consider Crane's characterization of the lieutenant. How is his character revealed? What are his dominant traits? How is his character related to the story's larger themes and ideas?
3. In the final paragraph, Crane writes, "And this is the story of how the lieutenant lost his arm." What exactly is the story? Why does the lieutenant stand "shamefaced" amid the tears of his sisters, mother and wife? What does the word "shamefaced" suggest?

4. Discuss Crane's descriptions of the wound. What is significant about the description? What symbolic role does the wound play? Why is the wound significant to the story or to Crane's purposes?

Theodore Dreiser, Old Rogaum and His Theresa

1. Describe the story's setting. What role does the setting play in this story? How is the setting revealed and described? What does it contribute to the story's themes and ideas?
2. Why does Dreiser use dialect for Mr and Mrs Rogaum's dialogue? What does it contribute to the story? What issues does it raise? What effect does it have?
3. Gender is a key concept of this story. What does this story reveal about gender, gender constructions, and power? How are these issues revealed and explored?
4. Is this story only about struggles between parents and children or is it about something larger?

Jack London, To Build a Fire

1. Discuss this story's connections with Naturalism. How does it illustrate characteristics of Naturalism?
2. Discuss London's juxtaposition of Nature and human nature.
3. Analyze London's choice of narrator and how it contributes to the presentation of character and theme.

PART II
Modern American Literature

Edgar Lee Masters,
Lucinda Matlock

1. Describe Masters's poetic style and form. What kind of poetic devices does he use? Does the style and form help reveal the poem's subject matter?
2. What do we learn about Lucinda? What does she reveal about herself and her life? How are these elements conveyed to us?
3. What is meant by the final two lines of the poem? How are these two lines connected with the rest of the poem?

Edwin Arlington Robinson,
Richard Cory

1. How does Robinson depict Richard Cory in stanzas 1-3?
2. Discuss this poem in relation to the concepts of appearances and realities.
3. What do the rhyme and meter contribute to the poem?

Edwin Arlington Robinson,
Miniver Cheevy

1. Examine this poem's rhythm and rhyme. How would you describe these elements? What do the rhythm and rhyme contribute to your understanding of the poem?
2. What does Robinson reveal about Miniver Cheevy? How would you describe him? What is the speaker's attitude toward him? Is this poem celebratory or critical of him?
3. Why did Miniver Cheevy love "the days of old," sigh "for what was not" and "call it fate"? How is the final line related to these and the other descriptions in the poem?

Edwin Arlington Robinson, Eros Turannos

1. What does "Eros Turannos" mean? How is the title connected with the poem? How is this concept addressed within the poem?
2. Who are the he and the she who are mentioned? What do we know about them? What is the relationship between them? How are they depicted or described? How is the "we" connected with the he and the she?
3. Analyze the poem's rhyme scheme. What is significant about it? What is revealed or conveyed through this particular rhyme scheme?

Paul Laurence Dunbar, Sympathy

1. Explain the relationship between the narrator and the caged bird. What is revealed about the relationship the narrator sees? What does this relationship reveal?
2. Examine Dunbar's use of imagery. What kinds of images are used and to what effect? How do the images help to develop themes?
3. What do you think is the nature of the prayer and the plea mentioned in line 19? Why does the narrator know why the caged bird sings? Why does the caged bird sing?

Paul Laurence Dunbar, We Wear the Mask

1. What does Dunbar mean by the mask? What is it a symbol of?
2. What does the use of the word "we" contribute to the poem? Who is the "we"?
3. Explain the significance of the line "We sing, but oh the clay is vile." What does this line add to the poem?

Willa Cather, Paul's Case

1. Analyze Cather's depiction of setting. How does she connect the interior and exterior settings?
2. Explain the significance of the following quotation as it relates to Paul's character: "In Paul's world, the natural nearly always wore the guise of ugliness, that a certain element of artificiality seemed to him necessary in beauty."
3. Describe how Cather uses music as a literary motif.

Gertrude Stein, The Gentle Lena

1. Repetition (or as she termed it, "insistence") is a signature feature of Gertrude Stein's style. What effect does this formal trait have on characterization in this story?
2. How does Stein convey Lena's innocence? How does Lena's innocence impede her? Help her?
3. How do cultural hierarchies based on gender, class and race affect the attitudes and experiences of the characters?
4. Is Lena depressed? Is this story a psychological portrait or sociological critique?

Amy Lowell, The Captured Goddess

1. Describe the poem's form. What is the significance of Lowell's poetic form? How does Lowell's use of formal elements help convey the poem's subject matter?
2. Throughout the poem, Lowell makes numerous references to color. What does the color contribute to your experience of the poem?
3. What is the Goddess? What is the narrator's relationship to the Goddess? How is the Goddess depicted?

Amy Lowell, Venus Transiens

1. Who is the "you" addressed in the poem? What is the nature of the relationship between the narrator and the "you"? How does Lowell use poetic devices to convey the nature of the relationship?
2. Describe Lowell's use of syntax and line breaks. What effect do the line lengths have? What is formally significant about the syntax and line breaks?
3. The editor suggests several interpretive possibilities for the title in translation. Which translation do you think best suits the poem?

Amy Lowell, Madonna of the Evening Flowers

1. Consider Lowell's use of nature imagery. What does this imagery contribute to the poem? Are these images well suited to the poem's subject matter?
2. Several words, images and phrasings are repeated. What is repeated? Why might these be repeated and what is the significance or effect of the repetitions?
3. Why is the poem called "Madonna of the Evening Flowers"? How is the Madonna image conveyed? Why is it important to the poem? Is it different from or similar to traditional associations with the Madonna?

Amy Lowell September, 1918

1. Lowell uses unusual similes and metaphors in this poem. Identify her most interesting uses of figurative language and describe how they contribute to the poem either in terms of form or theme.
2. Time is a central concept in this poem. It is used both as a specific subject and as an abstract concept. Explain the multiple ways in which time is addressed.

3. Analyze the line, "someday, there will be no war." What is significant about this line in terms of its placement and its thematic contribution to the poem?

Amy Lowell, New Heavens for Old

1. Throughout the poem, Lowell juxtaposes "I" with "they." Who are "they" and why is the "I" distinct from them? How is this distinction conveyed?
2. Analyze Lowell's use of repetition. What is repeated and why is it repeated? How does the repetition contribute to the poem in terms of form and/or theme?

Amy Lowell, The Taxi

1. There are different kinds of actions in each line. What does the stress on action suggest in this poem?
2. What is significant about the title? What work does it do in the poem? What does it contribute to your understanding of the poem?
3. Lowell's choice of figurative language encourages us to look at ordinary things in different ways. Explain the effect of Lowell's use of figurative language in this poem.

Robert Frost, The Pasture

1. Consider Frost's structural choices. How does he structure this poem? Why might he have chosen this particular structure for this subject matter?
2. As the editor notes, cadence and rhythm are important elements of Frost's works. Examine how cadence and rhythm function in this poem.
3. Lines 1 and 5, 4 and 8 have a repetitive structure. What does this repetition add to the poem either formally or thematically?

Robert Frost,
Mending Wall

1. Examine Frost's treatment of the wall as a subject and as an image. What questions or issues does it allow him to explore?
2. Explain the role of the wall in the context of the two neighbors. How are the two people's characters revealed through Frost's description of the wall and their responses to the wall?
3. Why does Frost repeat the phrase "Good fences make good neighbors"? How is that saying related to the poem or the two characters?

Robert Frost,
Home Burial

1. What is a narrative poem? How is this poem an example of a narrative poem? What happens in this poem?
2. Describe the relationship between the man and the woman. How does Frost depict this relationship?
3. Explain the significance of the grave? How does Frost use it?

Robert Frost,
After Apple-Picking

1. What is the setting of this poem? Why is he thinking about apples?
2. Examine Frost's use of sensory details. How do they contribute to the poem?
3. Analyze Frost's rhyme scheme. How does he use rhyme for effect.

Robert Frost,
The Wood-Pile

1. Much of this poem is concerned with the narrator's internal thoughts and the narrator's imagining of others' internal thoughts. What does this internal quality contribute to the poem?

2. Examine the woodpile as a central image. What function does it have in the poem? Is this an effective image? Why or why not?
3. Analyze the relationship between the internal and external settings. How do they inform each other? Why is this relationship significant to the poem?

Robert Frost,
The Road Not Taken

1. What is revealed about the narrator's character through his or her analysis of the roads and the choices he or she makes?
2. Explain Frost's use of rhyme and stanza. How do the rhyme scheme and the stanza structure help advance the poem's themes.
3. What do you think the narrator means by the statement "And that has made all the difference"?

Robert Frost,
Birches

1. This poem is entitled "Birches." Is this poem about birch trees or is it about something else? If so, what is this poem about and how is it related to birch trees?
2. Consider the formal and thematic significance of the line "But I was going to say when Truth broke in.. " What functions does this line have in the poem?
3. The final line in the poem is "One could do worse than be a swinger of birches." Examine Frost's construction of and/ or treatment of the "swinger of birches." What does it mean to be a "swinger of birches"?

Robert Frost,
'Out, Out—'

1. Do a close reading of the first fifteen lines. What kind of mood is set? How is this mood established? How does this mood relate to the remainder of the poem?

2. The title alludes to a particular passage from *Macbeth* and thus sets up expectations. How do the poem's rhythm and meter relate to these expectations? Does it affirm or challenge these expectations?
3. Consider the final five lines of the poem. How are the events conveyed? What poetic devices are used? Would you call these lines effective? Why or why not?

Robert Frost, Fire and Ice

1. Consider Frost's use of poetic devices. In particular, analyze his use of syntax and rhyme. How does he use these devices for effect?
2. Fire and Ice are alluded to throughout the poem. What is Frost suggesting through fire and ice? Is he using fire and ice metaphorically or literally?
  In line 6, the narrator writes, "I think I know enough to hate." Why is hate mentioned? How is it related to the rest of the poem? How is it related to fire and ice?

Robert Frost, Nothing Gold Can Stay

1. Observe Frost's use of rhythm, meter and audience. What is the effect of these elements on the poem? How do these elements relate to the subject matter?
2. What is meant by the line "Nothing gold can stay."? To what is gold referring?
3. Analyze Frost's use of punctuation at the end of the lines. What work does this punctuation do? How does it shape your reading or understanding of the poem?

Robert Frost, Stopping by Woods on a Snowy Evening

1. Why does the speaker stop to watch the "woods fill up with snow"? What draws him to this scene?
2. How does Frost create mood and what kind of mood does he create?

3. Examine Frost's rhyme scheme and discuss how he uses rhyme to create an effect or meaning?

Robert Frost,
Desert Places

1. Read this poem out loud. What do you notice about the sound of this poem? Does the sound of the poem contribute to your understanding of the subject matter or help convey the narrator's attitude toward the subject matter?
2. Loneliness is mentioned several times. How is loneliness described? What is this poem suggesting about loneliness? How does loneliness connect with the final stanza?
3. Reflect upon the relationship that exists between the external world the narrator sees and the mindset of the narrator. How is this relationship described?

Robert Frost,
Design

1. Scan the poem and describe how Frost uses rhyme and rhythm, punctuation and syntax for effect.
2. Connect this poem with another Frost poem about nature. How are they similar? What differences are there between the poems?
3. Explain the relationship between the final line and the rest of the poem.

Robert Frost,
Neither Out Far Nor In Deep

1. Describe Frost's use of rhythm and rhyme. What is the rhythm and rhyme scheme in this poem? What effect do these elements have on your experience of the poem and your understanding of it?
2. The water is a key element in this poem. What is its thematic function in this poem?
3. Examine the concepts of far and deep. How are they related to this poem? Of what are they representative?

Sherwood Anderson,
Hands

1. The narrator says, "The story of Wing Biddlebaum is a story of hands." Why are hands central to this story, Wing's story and Wing's character?
2. Describe how Adolph Myers became Wing Biddlebaum. Why does he change his name? How is this change in character conveyed?
3. Analyze Anderson's use of setting for thematic purposes. How does he use setting to convey mood or tone?

Carl Sandburg,
Chicago

1. Contemplate Sandburg's description of Chicago. What is significant about his choice of Chicago as a subject? What is significant about his depiction of Chicago?
2. Consider Sandburg's choice of formal elements such as syntax, line breaks, diction and rhythm. How do these choices help convey his sense of Chicago?
3. Examine Sandburg's use of repetition. What gets repeated? What is the effect of this repetition in terms of the subject matter?

Wallace Stevens,
The Snow Man

1. Explain Stevens's use of poetic diction and poetic devices. What language does Stevens use and what is the effect of this language? What poetic devices does he use and what are the effects of these devices?
2. What is the subject of this poem? What is being described here? What leads you to this conclusion?
3. Why does he call his poem "The Snow Man"? Explain the significance of the title.

Wallace Stevens, Sunday Morning

1. Describe how Stevens uses section breaks. Analyze his use of numbered sections and the order in which he places the sections.
2. Analyze Stevens's use of nature imagery, particularly images of birds and fruit.
3. Stevens uses language that refers to mythology and religion. What does this contribute to the poem's overall themes or effect?

Wallace Stevens, Anecdote of the Jar

1. What is the significance of the jar? What happens to it? Why? How does Stevens use it as an image?
2. Describe Stevens's style, form and structure in this poem. What do these elements contribute to the poem as a whole?
3. Analyze Stevens's depiction of nature. How is nature described in this way and why is he describing it in this way?

Wallace Steven, Thirteen Ways of Looking at a Blackbird

1. Analyze how Stevens uses the thirteen sections. What kind of relationships does he set up with these sections? What is the overall effect of these sections?
2. Examine the treatment of the blackbird in each section. Is it the same bird? Is it treated similarly or differently? What do these depictions of blackbirds reveal?
3. As the editor notes, Stevens observed that "Life is not people and scene but thought and feeling." Does this quotation apply to this poem? If so, how?

Wallace Stevens,
The Death of a Soldier

1. The editor cites Robert Pack who wrote of Stevens, "If a poem begins with a generalization, he will proceed to illustrate it, or, if a poem commences with a series of illustrations, it will end with a generalization." Examine this poem in the context of this quotation.
2. Evaluate the effectiveness of Wallace Stevens's choice of diction and imagery. Is it effective for the subject matter? Why or why not?
3. Is it significant that the subject of this poem is said to be a soldier. Why did Stevens include that specific detail?

Wallace Stevens,
The Idea of Order at Key West

1. Who is the "she" mentioned in the poem? What do we know about her? How is she depicted? What is her function in the poem?
2. Read the poem out loud. What does this poem sound like? How is this sound created through language and rhythm? What does the sound contribute to your understanding of this poem?
3. Why does Stevens mention "rage for order" and "rage to order" in the final lines? What does this repetition contribute to the poem? What does the shift from "for" to "to" do?

Wallace Stevens,
Of Modern Poetry

1. Analyze the relationship between the poem's first full sentence and the remainder of the poem.
2. Contemplate Stevens's use of "It has. . . " Where and why does he use this phrasing? What is achieved through its repetition?
3. Describe Stevens's choice of diction and imagery. What do the diction and imagery suggest about the poem and/or about the mind?

Wallace Stevens,
The Plain Sense of Things

1. As the editor notes, Stevens was very interested in the relationship between imagination and reality. Analyze this poem in the context of the relationship between imagination and reality.
2. What do you think is meant by the phrase "The Plain Sense of Things"? How is this concept addressed in this poem?
3. Stevens uses many words that suggest an absence (i.e., blank, silence, inanimate, etc). How do these words contribute to the subject of imagination?

Susan Glaspell,
Trifles

1. Both the men and the women are doing investigations of the situation. Compare the two investigations. How are they similar? How are they different? Whose methodology works best?
2. Discuss the play as a commentary on women and men. How does this play address the differences between men and women? The divisions between their lives? The relationships between men and women?
3. Mrs. Wright doesn't appear in the action, yet we learn a lot about her. How do the various characters present information about Mrs. Wright? How do the different points of view describe her? How does Glaspell use point of view for thematic purposes?
4. Hale says "women are used to worrying over trifles." What's meant by the title *Trifles*? What is "trifles" referring to? Is there irony in Glaspell's use of the word "trifles"?
5. Glaspell chooses to tell the story of the death using dialogue, the past tense and second hand sources. What does she achieve by using this kind of approach?
6. Do a character sketch of Mrs. Hale or Mrs. Peters. How is their character conveyed?

7. What is the symbolic significance of the bird?
8. What is the significance of the quilt? What role does it play? Why does it recur in the dialogue?

William Carlos Williams, The Young Housewife

1. Williams's poems have a very specific style. Using this poem, describe his style and show how his style is created through poetic devices.
2. How is Williams using language for effect in this poem? What kind of effect is created and how is it created?
3. This poem is titled "The Young Housewife." Examine Williams's depiction of the housewife. How does he address her as the subject of this poem? Is she the subject of this poem?

William Carlos Williams, Portrait of a Lady

1. Read this poem to yourself and then read it aloud. How does this poem change when read aloud? What elements create the aural effects?
2. Discuss what the title and the allusions to Fragonard and Watteau contribute to your understanding of this poem.
3. Analyze Williams's use of punctuation and repetition. What effect do they have on this poem?

William Carlos Williams, Spring and All

1. Who is the "they" mentioned in the poem? Support your answer with examples from the text.
2. Describe how Williams uses language and sound to create an effect. What is the effect and how is it created?
3. How does Williams approach nature? How does his diction convey his approach to nature?

William Carlos Williams,
To Elsie

1. The editor quotes Williams's memoir regarding his form: "I was trying for something." Apply this statement to this poem. What do you think Williams was trying for in this poem? How is this effect conveyed?
2. This poem addresses American and things American. How is Williams addressing America in this poem?
3. Analyze Williams's use of syntax, line breaks, and stanza form. What is notable about his use of these elements?

William Carlos Williams,
The Red Wheelbarrow

1. Examine Williams's use of line breaks and stanzas. How do they contribute to the poem?
2. Describe Williams's style. How is it similar to other poets of Williams's time? How is it different?
3. *What* depends on a red wheelbarrow glazed with rain water beside the white chickens?

William Carlos Williams,
Death

1. The editor notes that Williams was "extremely conscious of the arrangement of the words on the page and the relationship of words to white space." Apply this concept to this poem. How has Williams arranged the words on the page and what effect is achieved by this arrangement.
2. Who is the "he" in this poem and what is the narrator's tone toward him? How is tone created or conveyed?
3. Repetition plays a key role in this poem. What gets repeated and why is this important for this poem?

William Carlos Williams,
This Is Just to Say

1. Examine the effectiveness of Williams's style. Do you think this is an effective poetic treatment of this subject matter?
2. Williams separates the final four lines of the poem. Why might he have done this? What effect do those four lines have on your understanding of the poem?
3. What does this poem's form and style suggest about poetry and poetics? Does it support, alter or challenge your ideas about poetry and poetics?

William Carlos Williams,
The Dance

1. Find a copy of the Brueghel painting described in this poem. How does the poem inform the painting? How does the painting inform the poem?
2. Read the poem out loud. If you don't know the Brueghel painting, what do you imagine the painting looks like based on the sound of the poem. If you do know the painting, how is the sound of the poem connected with the painting?
3. Compare the form of this poem with "Landscape" which is also about a painting. How is it similar? Different? What is significant about the differences between the poems?

William Carlos Williams,
Landscape with the Fall of Icarus

1. In this poem, Williams alludes to Breughel's painting "The Fall of Icarus." What is the story of Icarus and what is Williams suggesting about this story?
2. The form of this poem is much different from Williams's other poem about a Breughel painting. Compare the two poems and suggest why Williams might have chosen the forms he did for each subject.
3. Williams takes note of the farmer in the field in Brueghel's painting. Why does Williams mention him? How is he central to Williams's poem?

Ezra Pound,
Portrait d'une Femme

1. How does the speaker characterize the woman? What is the speaker's attitude toward her? How well does the speaker know her?
2. What is the significance of the line "Your mind and you are our Sargasso Sea"?
3. How do the final four lines connect with the rest of the poem?

Ezra Pound,
A Pact

1. Who is Walt Whitman? Why is the narrator making a pact with him? What is the nature of this pact?
2. Examine Pound's use of word as an extended metaphor. How is it used? What is it used to convey? Is it an effective metaphor?
3. What is the significance of the final line? What kind of relationship is the narrator attempting to forge in this poem?

Ezra Pound,
In a Station of the Metro

1. Connect this poem with the Imagist tradition.
2. Why does Pound choose the word petals in the last line? What does this image suggest?

Ezra Pound,
The River-Merchant's Wife: A Letter

1. How does Pound use images to convey a narrative?
2. What is the nature of the relationship between the "you" and the "I"?
3. The title is "The River-Merchant's Wife: A Letter": how does Pound use the letter form in his poem?

Ezra Pound,
Canto I

1. As noted by the editor, "Canto I" is a loose translation of Homer's *Odyssey*. How is Pound conveying these events? What do his tone and diction reveal about these issues?
2. This poem is primarily narrative. Evaluate Pound's use of narrative strategies. Are they effective for this story and this form?
3. This poem is written in first person. What does this choice of narrator allow Pound to do? What is revealed about this character through the first person narrator?

H.D. (Hilda Doolittle),
Oread

1. Examine this poem as an Imagist work. What makes it an example of Imagism?
2. Consider H.D.'s choice of diction and the arrangement of the words. What is effective about her choices?

H.D. (Hilda Doolittle),
Leda

1. Describe H.D.'s treatment of this mythological story. What point of view is taken? How do this point of view and the other narrative choices affect this poem?
2. What effect does H.D.'s choice of diction and meter have on the poem? How do these elements work to create an effect?
3. Examine H.D.'s treatment of the swan. How is it constructed? Why is that significant to the poem or the subject matter?

H.D. (Hilda Doolittle),
Helen

1. Greece is mentioned in the first line of each stanza. Why is it mentioned and what does this add to the poem?
2. Investigate H.D.'s choice of diction. What kinds of words are used to describe her? What words get repeated? What is significant about this diction?
3. Explain the significance of the last three lines in relation to the poem as a whole.

Robinson Jeffers,
To the Stone-Cutters

1. Is Jeffers talking about stone-cutters or something else? Are stones and stone-cutters metaphors for something else?
2. In line 5, Jeffers mentions the poet. What is the relationship between the poet and the stone-cutters?
3. Time is a central concept in this poem. Describe Jeffers's treatment of time.

Robinson Jeffers,
Shine, Perishing Republic

1. In this poem, Jeffers uses juxtaposition in terms of theme and form. Analyze his use of juxtaposition. How does it contribute to this poem?
2. The editor cites the photographer Edward Weston who wrote of Jeffers, "His is the bitterness of despair over humanity he really loves." Apply this concept to this poem.
3. In the first line, Jeffers directly alludes to America. What is Jeffers suggesting about the nation? Is this poem a celebration, caution or criticism?

Robinson Jeffers, Hurt Hawks

1. Jeffers divides the poem into two sections. How are these sections different? What is the relationship between the two sections? How are these two sections used to develop the poem's themes?
2. Consider Jeffers's treatment of the hawk. How is the hawk described? What thematic concerns does he raise through the hawk?
3. In section I, the narrator is primarily concerned with "he." In section II, Jeffers uses first person. How are the "he" and "I" and connected? What does the use of "you" add to this relationship?

Marianne Moore, Poetry

1. What is Moore suggesting about poetry? What, according to this narrator, is poetry? What isn't poetry? What makes something poetry?
2. Moore makes several very conscious decisions about the physical placement of words on the page. How does the visual aspect of this poem contribute to your understanding of the poem?
3. Explain the final five lines of Moore's poem. Do you think the poem itself illustrates Moore's ideas about poetry? Why or why not?

Marianne Moore, A Grave

1. Examine Moore's poetic treatment of the sea. How does she reveal the nature of the sea?
2. As the editor remarks, Moore was concerned with "challenging and changing conventional forms of expression, phrase-making and imagery." How does this poem illustrate this concept?

3. Analyze the rhythm and meter of this poem. How does Moore use rhythm and meter to establish an effect? What is the effect that is created?

Marianne Moore,
To a Snail

1. Imagine reading this poem without knowing its title. What is your impression of this poem if you do not consider its title? Examine Moore's use of quotation marks. Where does she use them and to what effect? Why are some elements in quotation marks?
2. Is this poem an exercise in compression and style? Apply these concepts to this poem.

T.S. Eliot,
The Love Song of J. Alfred Prufrock

1. Examine Eliot's use of simile and metaphor and personification. How are these devices used and to what effect?
2. Analyze the effect of Eliot's use of repetition of phrases, words and sounds. Why might Eliot have chosen this particular effect?
3. Characterize the speaker. How does Eliot establish and convey character?

T.S. Eliot,
Tradition and the Individual Talent

1. Examine Eliot's discussion of tradition. What does he say is important or significant about tradition and literature? What, according to Eliot, should be the poet's relationship to tradition?
2. What is Eliot suggesting in the analogy about the platinum, the oxygen and the sulfur dioxide? How does this analogy relate to poetry?
3. Consider Eliot's discussion of personality and its relationship to art.

4. What, according to Eliot should be the role of emotion in poetry? What does he mean by "significant" emotion?

T.S. Eliot, The Waste Land

1. As the editor notes, "The Waste Land" was a primary text of literary modernism. Describe how "The Waste Land" embodies the tenets of literary modernism.
2. In this work, Eliot creates a unique and innovative structure. How would you describe the nature of this poem's form? Why is it formally innovative?
3. Examine Eliot's use of sections and section titles. How do these elements work together? What is the combined effect of these sections?
4. In numerous places, a first person narrator is used. Is this the same narrator or does the narrator shift? Analyze Eliot's use of narrator and perspective.
5. This poem has a strong aural element. Examine Eliot's use of rhythm, meter, repetition, onomatopoeia, and other aural elements. What do these sound elements contribute to the poem?
6. In this poem, Eliot assembles a wide range of styles, forms, topics, motifs, sounds, perspectives, voices, places and traditions. Identify these different modes. What is the collective effect of these modes when combined?

T.S. Eliot, Burnt Norton

1. Analyze the contributions of the opening epigraphs. What work do they do in this poem? What expectations do they establish?
2. Time is a recurrent theme, topic, and motif. Analyze the role(s) of time in this poem.

3. Throughout the poem, Eliot creates lines that are playful in terms of sound and sense and lines that build on and subvert each other. Find examples of this kind of playfulness and explain what these sections contribute to your understanding of the poem.
4. As the editor's footnote reveals, the title refers to the poem's central image, "the ethereal rose garden." Examine how Eliot uses this garden as an image. What themes or ideas are explored through this image?

Eugene O'Neill, **The Emperor Jones**

1. Provide a character sketch of Jones. Describe his past, his motivations, and the changes he undergoes.
2. Examine the concept of emperor in this play. How do different characters see the role of emperor?
3. Consider the silver bullet as a thematic device. What does it represent to Jones, Smithers, and Lem?
4. Describe the function of the shifting setting. What does the setting contribute to the play's themes?
5. Examine how O'Neill portrays the shifts in Jones' state of mind. How does he use staging devices to convey these changes?
6. What is Smithers's role in the play? What are his motivations and how is his character revealed by his dialogue and actions?
7. O'Neill provides copious stage directions. What do they suggest about his vision for the play?
8. Examine the narrative arc of this play. What thematic issues does its denouement reveal?

John Crowe Ransom, **Bells for John Whiteside's Daughter**

1. Analyze the depiction of John Whiteside's daughter. How does Ransom construct this character?
2. Why are there bells for John Whiteside's Daughter?

3. Analyze Ransom's use of rhyme scheme and meter. What is the overall effect of the rhyme and meter? How is this particular rhyme and meter connected with the subject matter?

John Crowe Ransom,
Piazza Piece

1. Compare the two speakers. What effect does Ransom achieve by having 2 speakers?
2. Examine Ransom's use of narrative strategies. What does this poem suggest about point of view and perspective?
3. What is the significance of the roses on the trellis? Of what are the roses symbolic? What do they contribute to the poem?

John Crowe Ransom,
Janet Waking

1. The editor notes that Ransom's poems are "simple-seeming but complex in organization and exploration of theme." Analyze how this concept relates to this poem.
2. Examine the mood of this poem. How is mood established? Do you think this is an effective mood for this subject matter?
3. Examine Ransom's choice of narrator. Who is the narrator? What perspective does this narrator offer us? How would a different narrator alter this poem?

Claude McKay,
If We Must Die

1. To whom do you think the "we" is referring? Do you think it is a general "we" or a specific "we"?
2. Who is the "common foe"? What does McKay reveal about this "enemy"?
3. Analyze the overall mood and tone of this poem. What effect do you think McKay was attempting to convey through this poem?

Claude McKay, America

1. Examine McKay's description of America. How does he describe it? What diction or imagery does he use to describe it?
2. How does McKay use the sonnet form for his purposes? How does he use form to advance the poem's central themes and ideas?
3. Compare this poem with another poem about America in this anthology. How are they similar? Different?

Katherine Anne Porter, Flowering Judas

1. Explain the significance of the title. What does it mean? How is it related to the story and its themes?
2. Compare and contrast Porter's construction of masculinity as represented by Braggioni and femininity as represented by Laura.
3. Examine Porter's treatment of revolution and revolutionaries. How and why are they significant to this story?

Zora Neale Hurston, The Gilded Six-Bits

1. Discuss Hurston's use of dialect. Why does she use it and what effect does it achieve? Why might she have chosen to use dialect in this story?
2. Compare 2 characters' views of and actions regarding money. What is the narrator's tone toward these characters? How are their motivations and characters established?
3. Explain the role of Slemmons in the story. What function does he have in this story?

Archibald MacLeish, Ars Poetica

1. What does "Ars Poetica" mean? Explain how this title is relevant to this poem.
2. In the final two lines, MacLeish writes, "A poem should not mean/But be." What does he mean by this statement and how does it apply to this poem?
3. Describe MacLeish's use of figurative language in this poem. Is his language evocative or effective for describing poetry?

Edna St. Vincent Millay, Recuerdo

1. What does "Recuerdo" mean? Why might this poem be called "Recuerdo"?
2. Read this poem out loud. What do you notice about Millay's use of rhyme, meter, rhythm and repetition? How does she create these effects?
3. Describe Millay's use of form and structure. How do stanzas 3 and 4 relate to the other two in terms of form and structure? How and why are they different?

Edna St. Vincent Millay, [I think I should have loved you presently]

1. What is the form of this poem? How does Millay use this form to advance the poem's central idea?
2. Examine the nature of the relationship the narrator describes. What are the narrator's feelings for the "you"? How does Millay use poetic devices to convey this relationship?
3. Analyze the poem's final couplet. How does it function formally and thematically?

Edna St. Vincent Millay,
[I, being born a woman and distressed]

1. In the opening line, the narrator refers to being born a woman. What do the two opening lines establish in terms of mood, theme, and subject?
2. What is the nature of the relationship described in this poem? What work does Millay's choice of diction do in terms of describing this relationship?
3. Examine the use of the sonnet form. In particular, how does the rhyme scheme help develop the themes of this poem?

Edna St. Vincent Millay,
Apostrophe to Man

1. What effect do you think Millay was trying to achieve in this poem? What stylistic choices help her achieve this effect?
2. Analyze Millay's use of syntax, line breaks, and line lengths. What is notable about the structure of the lines? How does the structure help convey the poem's subject matter?
3. What is meant by the final line? How is this line related to the poem as a whole?

Edna St. Vincent Millay,
[I too beneath your moon, almighty Sex]

1. What is the subject of this poem? How is the subject revealed through Millay's choice of imagery?
2. What is the "lofty tower"? How does it function as a central image in this poem?
3. What do you think is the "shadowy this and that/In me"? How are images of shadow and dark used in this poem? What do they contribute to the themes discussed?

Edna St. Vincent Millay,
Spring

1. There is a strong tradition of poems about spring. How is this poem related to this tradition? What kinds of associations does spring evoke? Does this poem live up to those associations?
2. The narrator notes, "I know what I know." What does the narrator know? How is this knowledge related to spring?
3. How would you describe the tone of this poem? How is the tone created? Why is tone relevant to this poem?

Edna St. Vincent Millay,
I Forgot for a Moment

1. The editor notes that this poem is one of Millay's "pointed political poems." Explain how this is a political poem.
2. Analyze Millay's use of forgetting. What is she able to convey through the narrator's forgetting?
3. In this poem, Millay uses juxtaposition and opposition. How do the juxtapositions and oppositions help to develop the poem's central ideas?

Dorothy Parker
General Review of the Sex Situation

1. What, according to this poem, is the "Sex Situation"?
2. Parker's poems tend to be very concise and condensed. Is this an effective style for this subject matter?

E.E. Cummings,
in Just-

1. Describe Cummings's poetic style. What makes his style different and innovative?
2. Explain the layout of the poem on the page. How does the poem work visually? Why is the visual layout significant to the poem?

3. How does Cummings use language, poetic devices and poetic forms to capture the essence of spring?

E.E. Cummings,
Buffalo Bill's

1. Examine Cummings's use of typography and placement of the words. What is effective about his placement of words?
2. In this poem, Cummings relies upon sight and sound for effect. Examine how he combines sight and sound in this poem. What effect is created?

E.E. Cummings,
the Cambridge ladies who live in furnished souls

1. Consider Cummings's depiction of the Cambridge Ladies. What is the tone toward them? Is it critical? Celebratory? Affectionate? Mocking?
2. Cummings uses language in fresh, new ways. Find examples of Cummings using language in ways that are new or fresh. What makes it new? What does this newness add to the poem or the subject matter?
3. Describe Cummings's use of syntax. How would you describe his syntax and what effect does it have on the poem?

E.E. Cummings,
next to of course god america i

1. Analyze Cummings's use of punctuation in this poem. Where is it used? Where isn't it used? What is achieved by his punctuation choices?
2. What allusions are embedded in this poem? What do these allusions contribute to the poem?
3. What is the thematic and/or formal relationship between the section in quotations and the final line?

E.E. Cummings,
if there be any heavens my mother will (all by herself) have

1. The editor quotes Cummings as saying, "the poem builds itself, three dimensionally, gradually, subtly, in the consciousness of the experiencer." Apply this concept to this poem.
2. Analyze the relationship between the poem's form and its subject matter. How is form used to describe heaven, the mother, and the father?
3. What do the parentheses contribute to your experience and understanding of the poem?

E.E. Cummings,
somewhere i have never travelled, gladly beyond

1. Discuss how the rose functions in this poem as a central image. How is it used? What does it convey?
2. Analyze the relationship the narrator describes. What is the nature of this relationship? How does Cummings use poetic elements to convey this relationship?
3. Describe Cummings's use of punctuation. How and where is it used and how does it contribute to your understanding of the poem?

E.E. Cummings,
anyone lived in a pretty how town

1. Who is "anyone"? What is the narrator suggesting about anyone and the town?
2. Examine Cummings's use of syntax and punctuation. What is the cumulative effect of the sentence structure Cummings uses?
3. Explain Cummings's treatment of anyone, someone, everyone, and noone. What function do these pronouns have in this poem?

James Thurber,
The Secret Life of Walter Mitty

1. Do a close reading of the first paragraph. What expectations or assumptions does it set up for the reader? Is this an effective opening for this story?
2. The editor notes that Thurber's definition of humor is "emotional chaos told about calmly and quietly in retrospect." Does this definition apply to this story? How? Why?
3. What is the thematic or structural significance of Mrs. Mitty? What does she add to this story? How does Thurber place her in the story for thematic effect?
4. Examine the story's final scenario. Do you find this an effective ending for this story? Why? Why not?

Jean Toomer,
Georgia Dusk

1. What is the subject of this poem? Why is the past significant to the poem and the men described in the poem?
2. Songs, singing and music are recurrent images in this poem. How are these images used? What is the significance of these images?
3. Examine Toomer's depiction of and description of setting. Explain why the setting is significant to the poem's themes and ideas.

Jean Toomer,
Fern

1. Describe Toomer's prose style in this piece. Is it similar to or different from other prose writings in this anthology? How would you characterize it?
2. Examine the narrative point of view. Who is the narrator? What are the narrator's biases or limitations in respect to Fern? Would you consider this narrator reliable?

3. The narrator writes, "men are apt to idolize or fear that which they cannot understand, especially if it be a woman. What insight into this story does this statement provide?
4. Explicate the final paragraph. How does it function as a conclusion to the story in terms of structure and/ or theme?

F. Scott Fitzgerald, Babylon Revisited

1. Explain the significance of the title. Why does Fitzgerald refer to Babylon?
2. Fitzgerald juxtaposes two couples— Lorraine and Dunc and Lincoln and Marion. What does he try to suggest through this juxtaposition? How do Charlie and Helen fit in with the comparison?
3. Fitzgerald alludes to some actual historical and cultural events. How is this story a commentary about the story's time and place?

Louise Bogan, Medusa

1. What does the title contribute to this poem? Why might Bogan have drawn upon this particular character for this poem?
2. This poem is told in first person. What does this choice allow Bogan to do in this poem? What do we know about this person?
3. What is the overall mood conveyed by this poem? How is this mood created and conveyed?

Louise Bogan, Portrait

1. Explain Bogan's selection of imagery. What are the various motifs suggested through the poem's imagery?
2. What expectations does the title create? Is this poem a portrait? If so, of what or of whom?

3. The editor comments that Bogan's poetry might be described as "hard, condensed, and durable." Is this description fitting for this poem? Why? How?

Louise Bogan, The Alchemist

1. What is alchemy? Why is alchemy significant to this poem? How is alchemy related to this poem?
2. This poem addresses issues related to body and mind. How does Bogan address concepts of bodies and minds?
3. This poem, like many others of hers included in this anthology, is very condensed and compact, yet it reveals many subtle nuances. How is Bogan able to be concise and subtle?

Louise Bogan, The Crows

1. Explain Bogan's use of crows as a central image. What ideas is Bogan able to convey through this image?
2. What is the relationship Bogan creates between the woman and the natural world? What does this relationship reveal about the woman?
3. Compare this poem with Bogan's poem "Women," both published in 1923. How are they similar and different in terms of structure and theme?

Louise Bogan, Women

1. What is the relationship between the natural world and the women described in this poem? What is meant by the line "Women have no wilderness in them"?
2. Select another Bogan poem in this anthology and compare the depiction of women in both poems in terms of desire, love, and physicality.
3. Explain the thematic significance of the final two lines. Thematically, how are these lines connected with the rest of the poem?

William Faulkner,
That Evening Sun

1. Examine Faulkner's choice of narrator. What does this particular narrator add to the story? How would this story be different if written from another point of view? Why might Faulkner have chosen this point of view?
2. Consider this story in terms of race, class and gender. What does this story reveal about this historical time and place?
3. What is the situation between Nancy and Jesus? What do we know about Nancy's situation? What don't we know? Why?
4. Describe the presence of the children in the story. What do they contribute to the work in terms of mood, narrative, character, and plot?

Ernest Hemingway,
The Short Happy Life of Francis Macomber

1. Describe Hemingway's narrative strategies. How are the events told? How is character established and described? How is conflict described and conveyed?
2. At several points, Hemingway alters the story's point of view. Whose points of view do we get? Why might Hemingway have chosen to offer these different points of view? What do they contribute to the story?
3. Examine the multiple functions of the hunt. What structural, narrative and/or thematic functions does it have?
4. Analyze the various relationships in this story. What are the different relationships? How are they conveyed? How does Hemingway describe these relationships? How do they alter or evolve in the story?

Hart Crane,
At Melville's Tomb

1. Explain the connection between the poem and its title. How is Melville related to this poem?
2. Consider Crane's use of diction and imagery. What is notable or significant about his use of language?

3. The editor includes Crane's own commentary on his poetry in the footnotes. What does this commentary add to your understanding of this poem? Is it useful?

Hart Crane, Voyages

1. Select one of the sections and analyze Crane's use of sea imagery. How is he using the sea for thematic purposes? Contrast this section's use of the sea with another section.
2. Who do you think is the "you" mentioned in the poem? What is the relationship between the narrator and the "you"? How is this relationship revealed through poetic devices?
3. Explore the motif of voyages. How is movement addressed in these sections? What are the voyages? Of what are the voyages suggestive?
4. How would you characterize Crane's style? What makes it distinctive?

Hart Crane, To Brooklyn Bridge

1. Examine Crane's treatment of the Brooklyn Bridge as a poetic subject. How is he addressing it? What do you think his purpose is in writing this poem?
2. The editor cites Crane as saying, "What I am really handling, you see, is the Myth of America." Explain this poem in the context of this statement.
3. Describe Crane's use of diction. How would you characterize his choice of words? What tone does his diction create? Why is this significant given the subject matter?

Sterling A. Brown, He Was a Man

1. Explain the thematic and structural function of the repeating fourth line. What effect does it have? How and why is it different in stanzas 10-12?

2. In the first four lines, Brown describes what the incident was not about and what he didn't do. Why does Brown use "wasn't" and "didn't"? What effect does this have?

3. Examine the tone and diction Brown uses to convey this disturbing subject. Analyze the effect and effectiveness of Brown's tone and diction.

Sterling A. Brown,
Break of Day

1. Read this poem out loud. What do you notice about the sound and rhythm of this poem? How are these aural effects conveyed? How do they contribute to the theme?

2. Analyze the narrative of this poem. How is this story told? Is this narrative structure effective for this topic? Why might Brown have chosen this particular mode of narration?

3. This poem and "He was a Man" addresses the racist violence in the first part of the twentieth century. Examine Brown's choice of literary strategies. How is he using poetic forms and strategies to make a social or political statement?

Sterling A. Brown,
Bitter Fruit of the Tree

1. Who are the "they" in the poem? What is the relationship between the "they" and the narrator's family? How is the nature of this relationship conveyed?

2. Consider Brown's treatment of bitterness. What is the tone toward the subject of bitterness? Why do "they" not want the narrator's family to be bitter? Do you think that the narrator is bitter or should be bitter?

3. Examine Brown's use of quotation marks. What do these add to the poem? Are they effective for the effect Brown attempts to create?

Langston Hughes,
The Negro Speaks of Rivers

1. Examine Hughes's use of rivers as a metaphor and/or a symbol.

2. Why has Hughes chosen to mention the rivers he has? What do they suggest?
3. Describe the "I." How does Hughes create the narrator? What is significant about the "I" in terms of the poem's themes?

Langston Hughes,
Mother to Son

1. The title conveys that this poem is about a mother's advice to her son. What advice is she giving him? How is this advice conveyed?
2. Analyze Hughes's imagery and use of figurative language. Do you find the imagery and figurative language effective for this subject matter?
3. Examine Hughes's use of form. How is it formally innovative? What does this form contribute to your understanding of the subject matter?

Langston Hughes,
The Weary Blues

1. In the title, Hughes alludes to the blues. How is the blues tradition related to this poem? Examine the formal and thematic significance of music to this poem.
2. Read this poem silently to yourself. Then, read it aloud. How is the poem different when read silently or aloud? Which way do you think is best and why?
3. Analyze Hughes's depiction of the musician. How is he described? What is characteristic of him? What role does he play in this poem?

Langston Hughes,
The South

1. How is the south characterized in this poem? What is the narrator's tone toward the south? How does Hughes use poetic devices to convey this tone?

2. Read this poem out loud. What rhythm and aural effects are created in this poem? What does the sound of the poem contribute to your understanding of the poem's subject matter?
3. Ponder Hughes's adjectives for the South. What kinds of words does he use? How does he use juxtaposition and contrast and why might he use these for effect?

Langston Hughes,
Ruby Brown

1. Examine this poem's structure in terms of the narrative. How does Hughes use stanzas to convey the narrative? How are the stanzas related to each other?
2. What is significant about the two questions and the placement of the questions in this poem? What do the questions and the implied answers reveal about the town in which Ruby lives?
3. Can this poem be read as a form of social commentary? If so, how?

Langston Hughes,
Let America Be America Again

1. What is meant by "Let America be America again"? How is Hughes defining America? Is there more than one definition?
2. Analyze Hughes's use of poetic structure. How does he use formal elements to help convey the themes and ideas within the poem?
3. Describe how Hughes uses punctuation and typography for effect. Examine his use of parentheses, dashes, italics, question marks, exclamation points, capitalization etc.
4. Consider this poem in the context of American nationalism and American nationalist discourse. To what other works does this poem allude? How does he use those allusions?

Langston Hughes,
Poet to Patron

1. What is the nature of the relationship that Hughes describes between poet and patron? How is the relationship conveyed?
2. How is Hughes addressing poetry? Is it a commodity or is it something else?
3. Analyze Hughes's use of structure. What does the structure contribute to your understanding of the poem?

Langston Hughes,
Ballad of the Landlord

1. Analyze Hughes's narrative strategies. What are all the different modes he uses to convey the story? Are they effective?
2. Examine the structural changes that occur in the poem. What work do these structural changes do in the poem?
3. Is this poem only about a landlord/tenant dispute? Or is it about something larger? If it's about something larger, what is this poem about?

Langston Hughes,
Too Blue

1. Read this poem out loud and describe the sound of the poem. How does the sound relate to the subject matter?
2. Compare this poem's treatment of the blues with another in this anthology by Hughes. How are they similar? Different?

Langston Hughes,
Theme for English B

1. Analyze Hughes's rhythm and use of repetition. How is it similar or different from other Hughes poems in this anthology? How does the repetition help to convey themes or ideas?

2. The instructor says "let that page come out of you--/ Then, it will be true." How does Hughes address the idea of truth?
3. Examine this poem as a commentary on race issues in America.

Langston Hughes, Poet to Bigot

1. What is the relationship described between the poet and the bigot? Why will they never agree?
2. The poem is built upon contrasts and differences. How does Hughes address these contrasts and differences both structurally and thematically?
3. Examine Hughes's description of power and his metaphors of stones and flowers. What do these metaphors convey?

Langston Hughes, I, Too

1. Discuss this poem as a statement about race, racism, and race relations in America.
2. Why does the narrator assert that "I, too, sing America" and "I, too, am America"?
3. What is the significance of the kitchen, the table, and company arriving?

Countee Cullen, Yet Do I Marvel

1. Examine this poem in terms of the sonnet form. How is it connected with that tradition?
2. Explain Cullen's allusions to mythology. What do they contribute to the poem's themes?
3. Discuss Cullen's treatment of race. Why does the speaker marvel at God's making a poet black and making him sing?

Countee Cullen, Incident

1. Explain how and where the poem's tone changes. Why is this change significant?
2. Why is this poem simply called "Incident"?
3. How can this poem be read as a commentary on race and racism? What is it saying about race and racism?

Richard Wright, Long Black Song

1. This story is dated 1938. Examine the geographic, historical, and social setting of this story. How is this story a commentary on that setting?
2. Describe Wright's treatment of race, class and gender issues. How does he address these issues? What is he suggesting about the relationships between races, classes and genders?
3. Violence, killing and death are recurrent topics in this story. Examine Wright's treatment of these issues. What is at the root of the violence?
4. In the final section, Silas says, "Yuh die ef yuh fight! Yuh die ef yuh don fight! Either way yuh die n it don mean nothin'. . ." Explain the significance of this quotation to the character of Silas and to the story as a whole.

Muriel Rukeyser, Effort at Speech

1. What effect is achieved through Rukeyser's use of spacing and syntax? What does this effect contribute to your understanding of this poem?
2. Describe the structure of the poem and explain how Rukeyser uses form to convey ideas about speech and relationships.
3. Analyze Rukeyser's use of repetition in terms of diction and form. Why are certain elements repeated? What do these repetitions contribute to the poem?

Muriel Rukeyser,
Suicide Blues

1. Analyze Rukeyser's use of figurative language. What kinds of similes, metaphors, and images are used? Are these effective for this particular subject matter?

2. Describe the recurrent image of voice. How is Rukeyser addressing voice and conveying the issues related to voice?

3. Explain the conflict present in this poem. What is the nature of the conflict? How does Rukeyser reveal the conflict's tension via poetic devices?

Muriel Rukeyser,
Poem

1. Rukeyser begins and ends with references to the war. Explain the significance of these two lines with the rest of the poem.

2. What does she mean by reconciling "ourselves with ourselves"? What might this entail?

3. Explain the significance of the title. How does it relate to her discussion about writing poetry?

PART III

American Prose Since 1945

Eudora Welty,
A Worn Path

1. Examine Welty's use of dialogue. How does Welty use dialogue to convey character, context and tone?
2. Provide a character sketch of Phoenix. What do we know about her? What are her dominant traits? What is this significance of her name in relation to her character?
3. How does this title connect with the story's themes? Is the worn path a suitable central image for the story?
4. Welty includes much description about the setting. What do the natural setting and the social setting contribute to Welty's development of character and theme?

Tennessee Williams,
Cat on a Hot Tin Roof

1. Examine Williams's choice of setting (geographical, cultural and historical) and his "Notes to the Designer." How does the physical setting work with the intellectual, emotional or thematic elements of the play?
2. The editor quotes Williams as saying, "Desire is rooted in a longing for companionship, a release from the loneliness that haunts every individual." Analyze this play in relation to this quotation.
3. Brick says, "but when we talk, it never materializes. Nothing is said." Discuss the themes of talking, voices, communication and speech. How does Williams treat communication between characters? What does the mode of communication reveal about this family and what does it contribute to the play's larger themes?
4. Explore the concept of "mendacity." What does it mean? Where is it discussed? How does it relate to the characters, the family and the play as a whole?
5. Select one of the characters and examine his or her relationships with the other characters. How is this character's personality and motivation conveyed? What is his or her role within the family?

6. Even though Skipper is not an actual character in the play, what is his role? What does he contribute to the events within the play? How does he relate to the characters in the play?

7. Examine the relationship between Brick and Big Daddy. How is this relationship different from others in the play? Why is it different? What does this relationship contribute to the play's larger themes?

8. Analyze Williams's stage directions. How do these directions shape the play or your understanding of the play? What do the stage directions contribute to your understanding of character or theme?

9. Consider this play's treatment of homosexuality. What does it reveal about the community within the play? Is this play still relevant in terms of its portrayal of homosexuality?

10. Examine the play's title. What does it mean to be a "cat on a hot tin roof"? Who calls himself or herself a cat? Who else might be a cat? How does this image relate to the play's larger thematic concerns?

John Cheever, The Enormous Radio

1. Describe the ideas of appearances versus reality in this story. How are these themes and ideas raised and addressed in this story?

2. Analyze the character of Mrs. Wescott. How does she change during the course of the story and why does she change?

3. What does the radio do in the story? How does Cheever use it as a plot device? As a symbol? As a conveyer of themes or ideas?

4. What is the significance of the final section of the story? How does it relate to the story as a whole?

Bernard Malamud,
The Mourners

1. Examine how Malamud addresses the concept of sympathy. How does Malamud create sympathy for characters? How do characters embody or avoid sympathy? How do characters change with regard to sympathy?
2. Provide a character sketch of Kessler. How does Malamud establish this character? How is point of view used? How does point of view affect how we view Kessler?
3. Analyze the concept of mourning and loss in relation to this story. How is Malamud addressing these ideas? What does this story suggest regarding mourning?

Ralph Ellison,
Battle Royal

1. Explain the significance of the introductory paragraph. What does it add to the story? What questions does it raise? Does its significance change after reading the story?
2. Why are the grandfather's words significant to the narrator? To the story's themes? Why does the narrator remember his grandfather's words at the end of the story?
3. Explain the function of the woman in the story. What does she contribute to the story? What connection does she have with the narrator and his story?
4. What does the Battle Royal reveal to the narrator about his community, about himself and about his future. How is the narrator changed by this event?

Grace Paley,
A Conversation with my Father

1. The story is a fictional story about writing fiction. How does Paley use the conversation as a commentary about fiction?
2. Paley does not directly describe the characters yet readers get a strong sense of who the two people are. How does she describe the two characters?

3. Explain the final line in relation to the debate between the daughter and the father regarding the story.

James Baldwin, Notes of a Native Son

1. In this story, Baldwin parallels the narrator's life history with the life of the nation. Examine the ways in which national issues are personal for the narrator and the narrator's personal issues are national.
2. Hatred, fear, and pain are recurrent concepts that the narrator addresses. How are these concepts addressed and how does the narrator come to terms with them?
3. The narrator tells the story retrospectively and much of this story is concerned with memory, reflection, and reconsideration. Explain how Baldwin's choice of narrator and narrative point of view affects the telling of this story.
4. Examine the thematic and formal function of the father. Thematically, what does the father contribute to the story? Formally, what is Baldwin able to do through the father?

Flannery O'Connor, Revelation

1. Analyze O'Connor's characterization of Mrs. Turpin. How does O'Connor reveal her character? Do you think we're meant to be critical of her or sympathetic toward her?
2. Examine O'Connor's treatment of race and class in this story. How are these issues raised? What issues about race and class does O'Connor raise and how are these issues raised?
3. Explain the significance of the hogs at the end of the story. How do they contribute to Mrs. Turpin's "revelation"?
4. What is Mary Grace's role within the story? What issues or conflicts does O'Connor raise through Mary Grace?

Martin Luther King, Jr.,
I Have a Dream

1. This is arguably one of the most important and memorable speeches of the twentieth century. What do you think makes this speech so important and memorable?
2. Rhetorical effectiveness meshes awareness of one's audience with awareness of one's purpose. What do you think King's purpose was in this speech? Who do you think his audience was? How effective is King's rhetoric?
3. Do a close reading of this speech and pay attention to his use of literary strategies. What do you notice about it in terms of form, content, and structure? Why might King have chosen these elements? Why are they effective choices?

Toni Morrison,
Recitatif

1. What does "recitatif" mean? How is this concept related to this story? Why might Morrison have chosen this particular title?
2. Morrison mentions that Roberta and Twyla are of different races but she does not specify who is white or who is black. Why might Morrison have left their races ambiguous?
3. Why is Maggie significant to this story? Why are the two characters so concerned with Maggie, her history, and their memories of what happened to her?
4. Race and class are significant parts of this story. Examine the lives and concerns of these two women in relation to larger social issues of race and class. How do these differences affect their lives and their relationship?

John Updike,
Separating

1. Describe Updike's description of the house and the setting. How does he use them to convey meaning or mood?

2. Examine Updike's choice of narrator. Is this an effective choice of narrator? What does this kind of narrator allow Updike to do? How would this story be different if told from another point of view?
3. Choose one character and analyze how Updike uses literary strategies to convey this character's personality.
4. Updike's story deals with a difficult emotional topic. How are these difficult emotions conveyed to us? What literary strategies does he use to convey these emotions?

Philip Roth, Defender of the Faith

1. What is the significance of this story's setting, geographically, historically, and socially? How is the setting related to the larger themes?
2. Provide a character sketch of Grossbart. What do we know about him? What narrative strategies does Roth use to reveal Grossbart's character? What do these narrative choices add to the story?
3. Examine the relationship between Max and Grossbart. What are the bonds? What is the conflict between them? How does each respond to this conflict and the bond?
4. Throughout the story religion and the army are juxtaposed. What is the nature of the conflict between them?

Amiri Baraka, Dutchman

1. Examine the character of Lula in the context of Baraka's comment that she is "not meant to represent white people . . . but America itself." How does Lula function as a representative of America?
2. Clay says, "We were talking about my manhood." Lula responds, "We still are. All the time." Examine the concept of manhood and how it is addressed in relation to the play as a whole.

3. Are we to read this play literally or metaphorically? If metaphorically, of what is it metaphoric?
4. Examine the final section of the play. Why is Clay stabbed? What do the conductor and the young man add to this scene?

Joyce Carol Oates, Where Are You Going, Where Have You Been?

1. Analyze the character of Connie. What does Oates mean by "Everything about her had two sides to it"?
2. How does Oates use the characters of Connie's mother and sister to explore her themes?
3. Oates is noted for her ability to create a sense of terror in her stories. How is she able to convey terror in this story? What strategies does she use?
4. How has Oates created the character of Arnold Friend? What does she say about him? How do the readers come to understand his character?

Raymond Carver, A Small, Good Thing

1. Examine the introductory paragraph and analyze how Carver sets up the baker's character, Ann's character and the relationship that ensues.
2. Explain the significance of the baker. What is his function in this story? What does he contribute to the themes and ideas in the story?
3. Examine the concept of the "compression of language" and relate it to Carver's style.

Toni Cade Bambara, The Lesson

1. What is "the lesson"? What is learned and what is the impact of this lesson on Sylvia?
2. How would this story be different if told from Miss Moore's point of view? Why might Bambara have chosen the narrator she did?

3. Sylvia notes that Miss Moore often says, "Where we are is who we are." What is the connection between this line and the story's larger themes?
4. Examine Bambara's use of setting. Why did she select the particular settings she did? What do the settings contribute to the concept of "the lesson"?

Terrance McNally, Andre's Mother

1. Analyze the presence of Andre's mother in the play. Even though she says nothing, why is she significant? Why is the play named after her?
2. Do you think this play is an effective form of social or political commentary? Why?
3. Examine the use of the white balloons and each character's treatment of them. What is revealed through each character's response to the white balloons?
4. Cal says, "Sorry, old friend. I blew it." Do you think Cal is right?

Bobbie Ann Mason, Shiloh

1. Mason titled her story after Shiloh, TN. Why did she choose this title and why is Shiloh significant to the story and the characters?
2. Discuss the role of houses in this story. Why is Leroy so determined to build a log house? Why is Norma Jean no longer interested in houses?
3. Leroy asks, "Is this one of those women's lib things?" Discuss the character of Norma Jean. Are her actions connected with feminism or the women's movement?
4. Analyze the changes Norma Jean sees in herself and the changes others see in her. Why does she change? What caused those changes? What are the effects of those changes?

Anne Tyler, Holding Things Together

1. Lucy, the story's narrator, describes rather ordinary everyday events. What is revealed in her descriptions? What do we learn about her from seeing things through her eyes?
2. Do you think Lucy is a sympathetic character? Why or why not?
3. Examine Lucy's various relationships with other people. What is the nature of her relationships? Do they change during the story? How? Why?
4. One of the story's central themes is power and control. How does Tyler explore these concepts?

Alice Walker, Everyday Use

1. Compare the characters of Maggie and Dee. How are they different and how does the narrator convey these differences? How does the mother view these differences?
2. Examine how the mother sees Maggie. How does her attitude change? What makes the mother see Maggie differently at the end?
3. Explain the irony and significance of Dee's statement that the mother and Maggie don't understand their heritage. Connect this statement with Dee's and Maggie's actions and statements.
4. Examine the symbolic and narrative role of the quilts. How does Walker use the quilts for thematic purposes?

Tobias Wolff, Say Yes

1. Examine Wolff's narrative choices. How might this story be different if told from Ann's point of view? How do you think she would interpret the events?

2. This story offers a brief snapshot of a marriage. What do we learn about this relationship? About the two individuals? About their interactions and understandings of each other?

3. Examine the final paragraph. How does this function as a denouement to the story?

4. Why do you think this story is called "Say Yes" rather than "Say No"? What does this title add to your understanding of the story?

Tim O'Brien, The Things They Carried

1. O'Brien repeats the phrase "the things they carried." What is being "carried"? What does it mean to "carry" something? Discuss the ways in which O'Brien uses "carrying" to convey themes or ideas.

2. Examine one character and do a character analysis of him based on what he carries.

3. Analyze O'Brien's treatment of Ted Lavender's death and how he conveys information about this death. What do O'Brien's narrative choices suggest about memory, truth and storytelling?

4. Explain O'Brien's story in the tradition of writing about war. How is it similar or different from other writings about war that you have read?

Leslie Marmon Silko, Lullaby

1. Memory, the past, and remembering are key elements of this story. Explore Silko's multi-layered treatments of the past and memory in this story.

2. Examine Silko's treatment of motherhood. How are Ayah's struggles as a mother conveyed? What issues are raised through Silko's treatment of mothers and children?

3. This story is about the life of an individual woman, yet it also raises questions about North American history and culture. Consider this story as a form of social commentary. What larger issues does this story raise?

4. This story is called "Lullaby." Examine the lullaby as an image and an object in the story. What thematic function does the lullaby serve in this story?

Amy Tan,
Two Kinds

1. Discuss Tan's story as a commentary on the American Dream.
2. Describe the relationship between the mother and the daughter. How and why are the perspectives different?
3. Analyze the effect of Tan's choice of narrator and point of view. What is achieved by her use of this point of view?
4. Explain the significance of the final section. Why does the narrator return to the piano as an adult? What has she learned about herself and her mother?

Alice Elliott Dark,
In the Gloaming

1. Examine the use of "the gloaming." What is it? Why might Dark have chosen it as a title? Why and how is it an appropriate image for the story?
2. Explain the significance of this line to the story: "Parents and children were all captive audiences to each other; in view of this, it was amazing how little comprehension there was of one another's stories."
3. What does this story suggest about this family's relationships with each other. Choose two family members and describe their relationship.
4. Explore Dark's use of internal and external settings. How are they related? How are they used for effect?

Louise Erdrich,
The Red Convertible

1. Discuss Erdrich's use of the red convertible as a central metaphor. What does it represent? How does this metaphor change throughout the story?

2. How does Erdrich convey Henry's character and the changes he undergoes?

3. Analyze the relationship between the brothers. What is it founded upon and how does it change? How does Erdrich convey this change?

4. Select another writing from this anthology that addresses the impact of war on individuals. Compare this writing with Erdrich's. How are they similar or different in terms of their discussion of war and the impact of war?

David Henry Hwang, The Sound of a Voice

1. Sound is an important element in this play. Explore sound as a thematic element. How is it used as a staging device?

2. The woman says, "The sound of a human voice – the simplest thing to find and the hardest to hold on to." What does she mean by this sentence? How does this sentence relate to the play as a whole?

3. Examine the use of flowers in the staging of this play. How are they used, of what are they suggestive, and how are they related to the themes of the play?

4. Analyze the relationship between the man and the woman. What does he want from her? What does she want from him? Do their motivations change in the course of the play?

5. The editor cites Hwang as referring to this play as "a tragic love story." Examine this label in relation to the play. Is it appropriate?

6. Investigate depictions of gender in the play. How is the play a story about gender?

7. Analyze the final stage directions in the play. How do these final actions conclude the play? What is the effect of these actions on your understanding of the play's larger themes?

David Leavitt, Territory

1. Analyze the relationship and level of understanding between Neil and Barbara. How does the presence of Wayne alter or change the relationship? Why?
2. What is the central conflict in this story? How do the characters' attempt to resolve it? Do you think this conflict is resolved?
3. In this story Neil attempts to understand Barbara as a mother, his mother, and also as an individual. What does this story suggest regarding identity?
4. Examine Leavitt's description of sexuality in terms of personal identity and family relationships. What role does sex play in Neil's negotiation of self and family relationships?

Suzan-Lori Parks, In the Blood

1. The editor notes that this play has been called "Parks's riff on *The Scarlet Letter.*" How is this play related to and/or different from *The Scarlet Letter*? What issues does it raise?
2. Examine this play as a metaphor for larger social issues. What issues is it addressing and how does it address them?
3. Parks uses a range of dramatic modes in this play. What is formally innovative regarding these modes and her use of them?
4. Examine Hester's various relationships with others. What does each relationship contribute to the play's larger themes? Combined, what do these relationships suggest?
5. Analyze Parks's stage directions and her use of "slightly unconventional theatrical elements." What is the effect of these stage directions?
6. Reflect on Hester as a character. How does Parks establish and convey her character? What function(s) does Hester serve in this play? What issues regarding race, class, and gender does she raise?

7. Examine Scene 9. What does this final scene contribute to the play as a whole? How does it relate to the previous scenes and the issues raised in them?

PART IV

American Poetry Since 1945

Robert Penn Warren,
Bearded Oaks

1. Who are the I, you, and we? What is the relationship described here? What is the nature and state of this relationship?
2. Do a close reading of stanza 7. What is suggested by the use of opposites and juxtaposition in this stanza?
3. Examine the oaks as a central image. How are they related to the speaker?

Robert Penn Warren,
American Portrait: Old Style

1. Analyze the structure of this poem. How does Warren use sections? What is the structural effect of these sections and their relationship to each other?
2. Describe Warren's treatment of time, memory, and history. How are these concepts addressed in this poem thematically and structurally? Why is it called "American Portrait"?
3. Do a close reading of lines 45-55. What do these lines add to the poem thematically? What concepts is he addressing and why might this section be placed where it is?

Robert Penn Warren,
Mortal Limit

1. Describe Warren's use of the hawk. What thematic and/or formal function does the hawk have in this poem? Is the hawk effective for these purposes?
2. What is meant by the poem's title, "Mortal Limit"? How is the concept addressed in this poem?
3. Throughout the poem Warren uses questions. What function do these questions have? What do the questions add to this poem?

Robert Penn Warren,
After the Dinner Party

1. What is this poem's tone? How is it created through literary devices? What does it contribute to the poem's subject matter?
2. This poem is about relationships and about the nearness and distance between people. What is revealed regarding the people in this poem? How are these relationships conveyed through poetic devices?
3. Examine the imagery used in this poem. What images recur? Why are these recurrent images significant?

George Oppen,
The Hills

1. Describe this poem's structure and use of poetic devices. What is the overall effect of Oppen's poetic choices (i.e. diction, rhythm, meter, syntax, imagery)?
2. The editor offers a definition of objectivism in the prefatory material on Oppen. Explain how this poem illustrates or exemplifies objectivism.
3. Compare Oppen's use of syntax, line breaks, and punctuation in each stanza. What are the similarities and/or differences? What is significant about these similarities or differences?

George Oppen,
Workman

1. What is the relationship between the narrator, the hawk, the carpenter, and the birds? How does Oppen forge a relationship between these four things in this poem?
2. As the editor notes, there is "little or no story" in this poem. What replaces narrative in this poem? What is it concerned with instead?
3. Why do you think this poem is called "Workman"? How is the title related to the poem as a whole?

Theodore Roethke,
Frau Bauman, Frau Schmidt, and Frau Schwartze

1. What is the narrator's attitude toward these three women? How are poetic devices used to convey the narrator's attitude? Where are the narrator's feelings revealed?
2. Roethke uses an additive structure and creates a list of activities and characteristics. What is the effect of this structure? What is achieved by using this list?
3. Roethke writes that these women "plotted for more than themselves." What is suggested by this line? How does it relate to the poem as a whole?

Theodore Roethke,
My Papa's Waltz

1. What is the "waltz" Roethke's speaker refers to? Why does Roethke choose the word "waltz"?
2. How does Roethke convey the nature of the relationships between the boy, the father, and the mother?
3. How do tone and diction help Roethke advance the poem's central image?

Theodore Roethke,
The Waking

1. Roethke uses repetition and is innovative in his use of language and phrasing. Examine his use of repetition and phrasing. What do they reveal regarding the subject matter of the poem?
2. Analyze Roethke's rhyme scheme. How is he using rhyme and what does his rhyme scheme contribute to the poem?
3. What is meant by "I wake to sleep, and take my waking slow" and "I learn by going where I have to go"? Why are these lines repeated?

Theodore Roethke,
Night Crow

1. Is this poem about the bird mentioned in line 1 or is it about something else? If it is about something else, what is it about?
2. Examine Roethke's use of diction. What kinds of words has he chosen? Combined, what kind of effect does the diction achieve?

Theodore Roethke,
I Knew a Woman

1. What do you think is the genre of this poem? To what tradition does it belong? How is it similar to or different from other poems in this tradition?
2. Analyze the allusions to Greek theater. What function do these allusions play in the poem?
3. Examine the structure of this poem. What do you notice regarding the rhyme scheme and the stanza structure? What do these structural elements contribute to the poem?

Theodore Roethke,
In a Dark Time

1. What do you think this poem is about? What do you think is the "dark time"? What leads you to this conclusion?
2. Examine this poem's diction and imagery. What is significant regarding these elements? What function do these elements have in developing this poem's mood?
3. This poem is written in first person. What does the narrator reveal regarding himself? How is this information revealed?

Charles Olson,
Maximus, to Himself

1. This poem uses a first-person narrator. Who do you think the "I" is in the poem? What do we know about this person?
2. Olson's diction relies on numerous abstract concepts and ideas. What is the effect of this very abstract language on your understanding of this poem?
3. Examine the physical layout of the poem. How is Olson using layout for effect? What is the effect of this particular layout?

Charles Olson,
Celestial Evening, October 1967

1. Analyze Olson's use of punctuation and syntax. What do you notice about his use of punctuation and syntax and how is this related to the poem as a whole?
2. What is the subject matter of the poem? How does Olson's use of poetic elements help contribute to conveying this subject matter?
3. How is Olson using external and internal settings? Is there a connection between these two kinds of settings in the poem?

Elizabeth Bishop,
The Fish

1. Examine Bishop's choice of diction. How does her diction reflect her attitude toward the fish?
2. What makes the speaker set the fish free? What does this say about the speaker? What does it say about the fish?
3. Explain the significance of the rainbow references in the final eight lines.

Elizabeth Bishop, Sestina

1. The sestina is a very specific poetic form. What is a sestina? How does Bishop's poem illustrate the sestina form?
2. What does this particular poetic form allow Bishop to do? What is the cumulative effect (either structurally or thematically) of the repetitions?
3. Examine the six words Bishop has chosen. Explain the relationships that emerge between these 6 words. Do the relationships change throughout the poem? How? Where? Why?

Elizabeth Bishop, In the Waiting Room

1. What is the significance of the *National Geographic* magazine? What did it contribute to her experience in the dentist's office?
2. Analyze what factors led the narrator to her new-found understanding.
3. What does the narrator mean by "you are an *I,*/you are an *Elizabeth,*/you are one of *them*"?

Elizabeth Bishop, The Moose

1. Much of the poem catalogues various sensory experiences of a particular place. Examine the function of place in this poem. Why is it important to the speaker and the poem?
2. The poem is called "The Moose," yet the incident with the moose happens quite late in the poem. Why might the moose have been chosen as the titular image? How does the moose relate to the rest of the poem?
3. Analyze Bishop's depiction of the natural world. How would you characterize her tone and mode of conveying nature?

Elizabeth Bishop, One Art

1. What is Bishop's speaker saying about loss and losing? Why does he or she call it an art?
2. Describe the speaker's attitude toward the "you." How is this loss related to other losses?
3. In the final stanza, Bishop uses a long dash and two sets of parentheses. Why does she only use these in her final stanza?

Robert Hayden, Homage to the Empress of the Blues

1. Discuss the poem's structure, particularly his use of "because." What does it add to the poem?
2. Provide a character sketch of Bessie Smith. How does the narrator regard her?
3. Hayden refers to "alarming fists of snow" and "the riot-squad of statistics." What do these images and ones like it add to the poem?

Robert Hayden, Those Winter Sundays

1. Describe the relationship between the narrator and the father. Why does the speaker describe it as he does? Is it significant that this poem is told in the past tense?
2. Examine the effect of the question in the final two lines. How does it affect the way you understand the rest of the poem?
3. Explore the father's work. Why does the narrator mention, "no one ever thanks him"?

Robert Hayden, Frederick Douglass

1. Read the poem aloud. What do you notice regarding its rhythm and meter? Is the sound of the poem significant to the subject matter? How and why?
2. Why does he call liberty "this beautiful/and terrible thing" and then "the beautiful, needful thing"? Why is liberty an important concept and how is its importance conveyed?
3. Examine Hayden's use of repetition. What is repeated and what is the effect of this repetition?

Dudley Randall, The Melting Pot

1. What is "the melting pot"? How does it function as a metaphor? Of what is it metaphoric?
2. Explore this poem in terms of race relations. How can it be read as social and/or political commentary? What is it saying regarding race relations?
3. Read the poem aloud. What do you notice about the rhythm? Why might Hayden have chosen this rhythm for this poem?

William Stafford, Traveling Through the Dark

1. Discuss how themes of life and death are addressed in this poem.
2. Analyze Stafford's choice of diction. How does it convey the speaker's thoughts about the deer?
3. What is the significance of Stafford's lines "I could hear the wilderness listen/ I thought hard for us all"?

Randall Jarrell,
The Death of the Ball Turret Gunner

1. Jarrell compares the gunner with a womb. What does Jarrell achieve by this comparison?
2. Compare Jarrell's language and imagery with another war poet's language and imagery.
3. Examine Jarrell's style. How would you describe it?

Randall Jarrell,
The Woman at the Washington Zoo

1. Examine Jarrell's use of syntax, repetition and assonance within the poem. What is the effect of his use of these elements on the poem?
2. Who do you think the speaker is and what does he/she reveal about him/herself? How is this information revealed?
3. Explore Jarrell's use of imagery. Is this imagery significant given the poem's subject matter?

John Berryman,
from The Dream Songs: 14

1. Examine the concept of boredom. How is it addressed in this poem? What is revealed about it? What is revealed about the narrator?
2. Why does the narrator believe he has no "inner resources"? What are the inner resources mentioned?
3. Study the poem's structure and use of punctuation. What effects are achieved through structure and use of punctuation?

John Berryman,
from The Dream Songs: 29

1. Examine the tone and sound of this poem. How is the sound of the poem related to the tone and content of this poem?

2. Examine Henry in this poem. What is Berryman suggesting about Henry? Is this depiction of Henry different from other depictions of Henry in other Berryman poems included in this anthology?

3. Do a close reading of the final stanza. What is it contributing to the poem as a whole? How is it related either structurally or thematically to the rest of the poem?

John Berryman, from **The Dream Songs: 40**

1. Read this poem aloud and examine Berryman's diction and syntax. What effect has he created through diction and syntax and how is this effect created?

2. What do we know about the narrator in this poem? What does the narrator reveal about himself? How is character suggested of revealed?

3. "Scared" is mentioned several times. Examine how fear is treated in this poem. What is the narrator scared of?

John Berryman, from **The Dream Songs: 45**

1. Examine the structure of this poem and the way the sentences are put together and ordered. What is achieved through the structure of the poem, the syntax, and the repetition of words?

2. The narrator refers to "they" throughout the poem. What do we know about the "they"? Does our understanding of "they" change during the poem? How and why?

3. Analyze the final line ("Henry nodded, un—"). What work does this final line do in the poem? How is it connected to the rest of the poem?

John Berryman, From **The Dream Songs: 385**

1. What is meant by the line "If there were a middle ground between things and the soul/or if the sky resembled more the sea . . ."? How is this line related to the rest of the poem?

2. Examine Berryman's use of "heavy," "heavier," and "daughter" and their placement in the poem. Why does he place these words where he does? What function do these words have?
3. Analyze the treatment of birds and flight. What do these images contribute to the poem? How are they addressed?

Robert Lowell, Mr. Edwards and the Spider

1. The title alludes to Jonathan Edwards's 1741 sermon. How does Lowell use this allusion to a Puritan sermon? What does he do with Edwards's sermon to make it relevant to the twentieth century?
2. In stanza 2, Lowell refers to "you." Who is the "you"? How is the "you" connected with the rest of the poem?
3. Analyze Lowell's use of the spider as the poem's central image. What is conveyed through the spider? What structural or thematic functions does the spider have in this poem?

Robert Lowell, Memories of West Street and Lepke

1. This poem is about remembering a very particular time and place. What does the narrator reveal about this time and place? What in the present causes this flashback to the past?
2. What is meant by the lines "These are the tranquilized *Fifties,*/and I am forty. Ought I to regret my seed time?"
3. Examine Lowell's collection of memories. What is remembered and what is significant in these memories?

Robert Lowell, Skunk Hour

1. Examine the various characters in this poem. Who is described in this poem? What does this assembly of characters contribute to the mood and idea of this poem?

2. In stanza 5 the poem focuses on the first person. What does this switch reveal? How are the subsequent stanzas related to the previous one? What does the narrator reveal about him/herself?
3. The poem is called "Skunk Hour" and the skunk is the final image of the poem. Why has Lowell drawn so much attention to the skunk and skunk hour? How are they related to the poem's themes and ideas?

Robert Lowell, Night Sweat

1. The editor refers to this poem as an "intense, frightening work." What makes this work "intense and frightening"?
2. Examine the diction chosen in this poem. Taken together, what images or body of images does the diction create? Why is this body of images significant to the poem as a whole?
3. Analyze the central image of the night sweat? Are we to read this literally? Metaphorically? Both?

Robert Lowell, For the Union Dead

1. How and why does Lowell link the Union Dead and the Aquarium? How do these images work together?
2. Why does this monument stick "like a fishbone/ in the city's throat"?
3. What is the speaker's attitude toward the monument? How does his diction convey his tone?

Gwendolyn Brooks, We Real Cool

1. Sound is a key part of this poem. How does Brooks create rhythm? What kind of rhythm does she create?
2. Examine how Brooks uses repetition for effect. Why might she have used repetition in this poem?
3. Relate this poem to another poet who uses sound. How are these poems similar or different?

Gwendolyn Brooks,
Martin Luther King, Jr.

1. Examine the figurative language Brooks uses to describe Martin Luther King, Jr. What does she say he is and what is significant about her descriptions?
2. Analyze Brooks's stylistic choices and structural innovations. How does her use of poetic devices help underscore her ideas about Martin Luther King, Jr.?
3. Look at the final three lines of the poem with regard to form and structure. Are these three lines an evocative ending for this particular poem? What do these lines contribute to the overall effect of the poem?

Lawrence Ferlinghetti,
Constantly Risking Absurdity

1. Examine the poem in terms of the Beat movement. How is the poem related in terms of theme, form, and/or subject matter to the Beats?
2. Study Ferlinghetti's use of syntax and the typographical layout of this poem. How is Ferlinghetti using these elements for effect and what effect is achieved?
3. Ferlinghetti offers the simile "the poet like an acrobat." How is the poet like an acrobat? How does Ferlinghetti play with the image of the poet in this poem? What is he suggesting about poetry and the poet?

Robert Duncan,
Often I Am Permitted To Return to a Meadow

1. Examine the structure of this poem. What is stylistically innovative about his use of form? How would you describe his form?
2. Analyze the image of the meadow. How is Duncan using the meadow and what is he doing with it?
3. The mind and imagination are central concepts in this poem. Why? How are they addressed and why are they significant to this poem?

Robert Duncan, Interrupted Forms

1. Analyze Duncan's use of syntax and line breaks. What is notable about these elements and what effect does he achieve through his use of them?
2. Seeing, looking, and perceiving are significant concepts in the poem. Where does Duncan address them and how are they addressed?
3. The poem is called "Interrupted Forms" and "interrupted" is mentioned at several points in the poem. Why is interruption an important concept? How is it relevant to this poem?

Richard Wilbur, Years-End

1. Analyze Wilbur's rhyme and meter. How does he use these for effect?
2. Explain the significance of the phrase "There was perfection in the death of ferns."
3. Compare Wilbur's description of winter with another poet's (i.e., Frost). How are they similar? Different?

Richard Wilbur, Love Calls Us to the Things of This World

1. Wilbur makes several references to the soul. What is conveyed about the soul? How is the soul addressed thematically and/or formally?
2. How does Wilbur juxtapose the mundane, earthly world with the heavenly world? Why is this juxtaposition significant to the poem?
3. Wilbur twice includes material in quotation marks. Why might he have used this device and what does it add to the poem?
4. Compare the depiction of the afterlife in this poem with that of another poem in this anthology.

James Dickey,
Drowning with Others

1. Examine Dickey's use of imagery. What are the dominant images in this poem? How is Dickey using these images for effect?
2. Analyze Dickey's references to the sea. Why is the sea an important concept and image for this poem?
3. Why might this poem be called "Drowning with Others"? What is suggested by this title? How is the title related to the poem?

James Dickey,
The Lifeguard

1. Why might Dickey have chosen to write this poem in first person? What does this narrative point of view allow Dickey to do?
2. The image of the moon is repeated throughout the poem. What is the effect of this repeated image? Does the image change or reinforce itself over the course of the poem?
3. Examine the narrator's "defeat," which forms the central event of the poem. How does the narrator view this event?

James Dickey,
The Heaven of Animals

1. Describe how Dickey depicts the heaven of animals. What is it like?
2. What does the speaker say is the animals' "reward"? What is at the "cycle's center"?
3. Compare the depiction of the afterlife with another poet.

Mitsuye Yamada,
To the Lady

1. Yamada uses lists and repetition to achieve a particular effect. What is listed? What is repeated? What do the lists and repetition add to this poem?
2. Why is this poem addressed to the Lady in San Francisco?
3. Yamada uses "I" and "you" strategically. How, where and why does she use "I," "you," "we," and "all"?

Denise Levertov,
In Mind

1. Who are the women described in this poem? What is the narrator suggesting about them? What judgments is the narrator making?
2. In two places, Levertov uses long dashes. Why might she have placed them here? What do they add to the poem?
3. Examine Levertov's structure. How is she using poetic form? What is significant about her poem's form? What work is it doing in the poem?

Denise Levertov,
September 1961

1. What is the overall mood of the poem? How is the mood created? Is this mood appropriate for this subject matter?
2. Levertov uses the image of having "words in our pockets." What is meant by this phrase? How is it significant for this particular poem?
3. Who are "they" and who are "we"? What are the "road" and the "sea"? How are these four elements connected? How do they relate to September 1961?

Denise Levertov,
What Were They Like?

1. Examine Levertov's structure. How is this poem structured? What does this particular structure contribute to this poem? Do you find it effective?
2. Throughout this poem, Levertov makes numerous juxtapositions, often between the beautiful and the horrific. Find examples of these juxtapositions. How does she use juxtaposition and why might she have chosen these images?
3. What is the historical context of this poem? Can this poem be read as a form of social commentary? How? Why?

Denise Levertov,
Zeroing In

1. The opening line features the first speaker saying, "I am a landscape." How is landscape being used as a metaphor in this poem? How is it being used metaphorically and what does it reveal?
2. In line 23, the female speaker makes reference to "it." What is "it"? Is "it" a figurative or literal thing?
3. What is the dog's function in this poem? How is she related to the landscapes the speakers describe?

Denise Levertov,
Salvator Mundi: Via Crucis

1. Who is the "he" mentioned in this poem? What do we know about him and how is information about him revealed?
2. Levertov mentions humanness and human a number of times. Why is this an important concept for this poem? How is it addressed?
3. What was, according to this poem, "Incarnation's heaviest weight"? What does this line mean?

A.R. Ammons,
Corsons Inlet

1. Examine this poem's form in terms of typology. How does this poem appear on the page? Why might Ammons have chosen this particular layout for the lines of this poem?
2. Ammons writes, "I allow myself eddies of meaning," "I have reached no conclusions," and "I make/ no form of/ formlessness." Discuss Ammons's treatment of form and meaning.
3. Analyze the setting of this poem and Ammons's treatment of this space. Consider it both thematically and structurally. How is Corsons Inlet connected with the poem and or poetry in general?

James Merrill,
An Urban Convalescence

1. Merrill's narrator refers to his own illness as well as the "sickness of our time." Examine the connections between the individual and the world at large, and between the inner and outer world.
2. Memory and the past are concepts addressed herein. Describe Merrill's treatment of the past and the process of remembering.
3. Analyze Merrill's treatment of New York as both subject and object. How does he describe it as a subject? How does he use it as a subject of poetic inquiry?

James Merrill,
The Broken Home

1. Merrill referred to his poetry as "Chronicles of love and loss." Examine Merrill's treatment of these concepts within this poem.
2. Merrill conveys a wide range of scenes and tableaux. How are these scenes and tableaux connected? What is the cumulative effect of these scenes on the poem?

3. Examine how Merrill conveys and interrogates the titular concept of "the broken home" through different narrative strategies and perspectives. What strategies and perspectives does he use?

Robert Creeley,
For Love

1. How would you characterize Creeley's use of syntax, line breaks, and stanzas? How do these choices affect your experience of the poem? What is the effect of these choices on the poem?
2. The final two lines of this poem are "Into the company of love/ it all returns." What is conveyed by this phrase and how does it relate to the rest of the poem?
3. Love is the central topic of this poem. Examine Creeley's treatment of love. What issues does he raise about love?

Robert Creeley,
The Messengers

1. The poem's title is "The Messengers." Who do you think are the messengers and of what are they messengers? What is the message?
2. In line 14, Creeley writes, "It raises the world." What do you think the "it" is? Support your answers with specifics from the text.
3. Using this poem as an example, how would you describe Creeley's style?

Robert Creeley,
For No Clear Reason

1. What do you think is the subject of this poem? What is "the fright"?
2. Who or what is "laughing, laughing at me" and why?
3. Why do you think there is "no clear reason"?

Robert Creeley,
The Birds

1. What is the relationship between the birds and the narrator? What issues is the narrator able to explore through the birds? Do you think the subject of the poem is the bird or the narrator?
2. Why do you think the narrator says, "the birds,/ no matter they're not of our kind, seem most like us here." Why are they "most like us"?
3. Examine the poem's structure. How are structural elements used for effect or emphasis? What do you think is the desired effect?

Robert Creeley,
Fathers

1. Read this poem out loud. What do you notice about the sound of this poem? What elements contribute to the sound? Is the sound effective for the subject matter?
2. This poem contains very few verbs. What is the effect of the absence of verbs? Why might have Creeley have chosen to write in this style.
3. Consider the last seven lines and do a close reading of these lines. What do you notice about Creeley's diction? What is the effect achieved by the word choice? Why is his diction significant for the poem?

Allen Ginsberg,
Howl

1. This poem was innovative and highly influential both formally and intellectually. What makes it innovative? Why do you think it was so influential?
2. This poem is peppered with allusions to people, places, and events. What kind of allusions does he use? How does he use these allusions? To what end are these allusions used?

3. The editor cites critic Helen Vendler who suggests William Blake, Walt Whitman, Ezra Pound, and William Carlos Williams are influences on Ginsberg. Where do you see their influences in this poem?
4. The editor cites Ginsberg as saying that poetry is "the outlet for people to say in public what is known in private." Examine this poem in the context of the public and private.

Frank O'Hara
To The Harbormaster

1. In his discussion of harbors, ships, and moorings, is O'Hara being figurative or literal?
2. The narrator refers to an "I" and a "you." What is the relationship between the I and the you? What is the narrator's attitude toward the "you"?
3. What is the central conflict within this poem? How is the conflict conveyed? Is it resolved?

Frank O'Hara,
In Memory of My Feelings

1. O'Hara's narrator uses a first person narrator yet challenges the idea of a single unified self. What is meant by "my transparent selves"? How is the idea of "self" explored in this poem thematically or formally?
2. Consider O'Hara's use of sections. How are the five sections related? What is achieved through the use of these sections?
3. Painter Jasper Johns created a painting based on this poem. Either find a copy of this image and discuss how Johns translates the poem into a visual form or discuss how one might make this poem into a visual work.
4. Why is this poem called "In Memory of My Feelings." How and why is this poem a memorial?

Frank O'Hara,
The Day Lady Died

1. How does O'Hara use time and chronology? What effects does this use of time have on the poem?
2. How does he use language, imagery, syntax and rhythm to create immediacy?
3. Why does O'Hara refer to the death of Billie Holliday? What does this add to the poem?

Galway Kinnell,
The Porcupine

1. Each of the seven sections is distinct. What is achieved through Kinnell's use of sections? Why might he have chosen this form? How are the sections ordered or structured?
2. The editor cites Kinnell as saying, "Poems about other creatures may have political and social implications for us." Do you think this poem has political and social implications? If so, what are they?
3. Who is the "I" mentioned in this poem and how is the "I" related to the porcupine? How is the "I" related to the rest of the poem?

John Ashbery,
Illustration

1. There are two parts to this poem. What is the relationship between the two parts? Why might Ashbery have chosen this two-part structure?
2. Examine the novice's speech. What does she say? What does she want? How are her desires and her words related to the rest of the poem?
3. What is meant by the first three lines of section II? Why does Ashbery discuss "we" in the second part? Why are "we" important to this section?

John Ashbery,
The Lament Upon the Waters

1. What is meant by the phrase, "The problem isn't how to proceed/ But is one of being"? How is this line connected with the ideas explored in this poem?
2. Examine Ashbery's choice of imagery. What kinds of images are used and what do they contribute to the poem?
3. The editor cites critic David Perkins who remarks that Ashbery's "envisionings of reality are not merely provisional; they transform themselves and disappear in the very process of being proposed." Apply this concept to this poem and analyze Ashbery's depictions of reality.

W.S. Merwin,
For the Anniversary of My Death

1. How does the speaker address death? What does death represent to him? What is his attitude toward death? How is this attitude conveyed through poetic devices?
2. Why does Merwin break the stanza at line 5? What is the relationship between stanzas 1 and 2?
3. Explain the significance of the wren. How does the wren function as a symbol in this poem?

W.S. Merwin,
For a Coming Extinction

1. The editor cites Merwin who noted, "Our importance is based on a feeling of responsibility and awareness of all life." How are the concepts of responsibility, importance, and awareness related to this poem?
2. Consider Merwin's use of poetic form. What is the effect of his choices of form? How does the form work with the poem's content?
3. Analyze the poem's final two lines. Is Merwin being ironic? Is irony a part of this poem?

W.S. Merwin,
September Plowing

1. Examine Merwin's depiction of the natural world. What poetic strategies does he use to convey the natural world?
2. The title and the end of the poem refer to autumn. What is the narrator suggesting about autumn? How is it described? How is autumn related to the rest of the poem?
3. Analyze Merwin's use of poetic form and structure. How does this poem's form connect with the poem's subject matter?

James Wright,
Autumn Begins in Martins Ferry, Ohio

1. Wright takes a particular time and place and uses it as a spark for meditation. What insights emerge from the narrator's consideration of this time and place?
2. Examine Wright's choice of diction in the first two stanzas. How does the diction shape the tone of the poem? What issues are raised? How is this tone connected with the remaining stanzas?
3. Describe the function and placement of the word "Therefore." Why are the final three lines preceded by this word?

James Wright,
To the Evening Star: Central Minnesota

1. As the editor notes, Wright was often concerned with the relationship between the self and nature, the speaker and the landscape. Examine how Wright explores these relationships in this poem.
2. Analyze Wright's treatment of the natural world. What is the tone in this poem? What poetic strategies does he use to convey this relationship and establish this tone?
3. Who do you think the "you" is in this poem? What is the function of the "you" in this poem?

James Wright, A Blessing

1. Analyze Wright's poetic treatment of the two ponies. How does he describe them? What is significant about his description?
2. What is this poem's overall tone? How is the tone established and why is it significant for this poem?
3. The editor cites critic David Pink who characterized Wright as a "poet of epiphany." Do you think this statement is an accurate characterization of Wright based on this poem?

Philip Levine, Starlight

1. This poem explores a relationship between the narrator and his father. Examine the use of the first person narrator. What is the narrator able to reveal? How does this narrator convey this relationship?
2. Voice is mentioned numerous times in this poem. How is voice an important concept for this poem? What does it contribute to the poem? What does it contribute to your understanding of the poem?
3. Lights of various kinds are mentioned throughout the poem. What kinds of light are mentioned? How is light significant to the poem and its subject matter?

Philip Levine, The Mercy

1. Levine plays with the concept of mercy and uses it in several different contexts. Explain how Levine uses mercy and how it relates to the subject matter.
2. Analyze Levine's characterization of his mother. How is she described? What is Levine trying to convey through his depiction of her?
3. Levine's poem is about a common American experience. What is he suggesting about the experience of immigration. How does he convey this experience?

Anne Sexton,
The Truth the Dead Know

1. Explain the connection between the poem's dedication and the poem's themes and ideas. How is the poem connected with the dedication?
2. Analyze Sexton's discussion of death and truth. How are they related? How is this relationship conveyed?
3. What is the significance of Sexton's use of stones? What work do they do in the poem?

Anne Sexton,
Sylvia's Death

1. In this poem, Sexton describes Sylvia Plath's suicide. What is Sexton attempting to convey about this subject? What poetic strategies is she using to reveal these ideas?
2. Examine the structure of this poem. Consider line lengths, punctuation, and use of parentheses. Why is the structure important to this poem?
3. The editor cites Sexton as saying, "Poetry should be a shock to the senses. It should hurt also." Do you think this poem illustrates Sexton's statement? How? Where and why?

Adrienne Rich,
Storm Warnings

1. Consider the use of internal and external settings. How does Rich explore both settings? What does she suggest is the relationship between the two settings?
2. Time is a recurrent motif in this poem. How is time used? What is Rich suggesting about time?
3. Rich writes, "These are the things that we have learned to do." What have we learned to do and why?

Adrienne Rich,
Diving Into the Wreck

1. Examine Rich's use of diction. What does her word choice reveal about her speaker's attitude toward the subject?
2. What appeals to the speaker about the wreck? Why is she drawn to the wreck itself and not the story of the wreck?
3. What does Rich mean by "The words are purposes/ The words are maps"?

Gary Snyder,
Riprap

1. What is "riprap"? How is this word connected with the poem? How does Snyder use "riprap" in the poem?
2. How is Snyder using words as an abstract concept in his poem and as a vital component of poetry? Does the form of his poem relate to his description of words within the poem?
3. Explain Snyder's depiction of the natural world. What is he suggesting about this world and how are his ideas conveyed through poetic devices?

Gary Snyder,
August on Sourdough, a Visit from Dick Brewer

1. Analyze Snyder's structure. Consider line breaks and the typographical layout of the poem. What do the structure and layout contribute to your understanding of the poem?
2. Consider the setting of the poem. How is Snyder using a range of poetic devices to convey this particular setting?

Gary Snyder
Ripples on the Surface

1. Read this poem out loud. What do you notice about how this poem sounds? What role does the sound of this poem have in the experience of reading and understanding this poem?

2. Examine the physical structure and layout of this poem. How is the poem's subject reflected in the way it appears on the page?
3. What is suggested by the line, "Nature, not a book, but a *performance,* a/ high old culture"? How is this line connected with the rest of the poem?

Sylvia Plath, Morning Song

1. What is the subject of this poem and the narrator's tone toward it? What poetic devices is Plath using to convey this subject matter and tone?
2. Plath uses numerous similes and metaphors. Select 2 or 3 similes and metaphors and examine how Plath is using figurative language for effect.

Sylvia Plath, Lady Lazarus

1. Why does Plath use the Nazi and Holocaust references? How does she use them in the poem? What do they contribute to her themes and ideas?
2. What is the "it" Plath describes? How does she show us what it is without telling us?
3. Examine Plath's use of metaphor and allusion. How does she use these elements for effect? What is the effect achieved?

Sylvia Plath, Ariel

1. What is the subject of this poem? How is this poem's subject matter revealed?
2. Analyze Plath's choice of imagery. What kinds of images does she use in this poem and what is revealed through her images? What do the images contribute to the poem?
3. Explore the form of this poem. What are these formal elements contributing to your understanding of the poem? How do they shape your reading of the poem?

Sylvia Plath,
Daddy

1. How does Plath characterize or convey the character of the father?
2. Explain Plath's references to Germans and Jews. How does she use these groups to convey theme?
3. Describe the parent/child relationship depicted in this poem.

Linda Pastan,
Marks

1. Explain the narrative structure of this poem. What is the effect of Pastan's narrative strategy?
2. In this poem, Pastan provides a different take on marks and grading. How is she building upon and manipulating common assumptions about marks?
3. What work do the two final lines do in this poem? How else might Pastan have ended this poem? What does this particular ending do in relation to the previous lines?

Amiri Baraka,
A Poem for Black Hearts

1. Examine Baraka's poetic treatment of Malcolm X. How is he describing Malcolm X? What kind of diction and imagery does he use?
2. Consider Baraka's poetic form. What are the notable features of his form? Why might Baraka have made the formal choices he did? What effect do you think he was trying to achieve?
3. Can this poem be read as a political commentary? If so, how is it political and what is it suggesting?

Mary Oliver,
The Black Snake

1. Oliver uses the snake as a way to ponder mortality. What does the speaker convey about mortality?

2. Explore Oliver's use of punctuation and typography. How do these elements inform your reading of the poem?

3. In the last two stanzas, Oliver makes use of the "It is" construction. Why does she repeat this phrase? To what does the "it" in the sentence refer?

Mary Oliver,
Hawk

1. Examine the physical layout of this poem. How would you describe its visual form? How is the visual form related to the poem's subject matter?

2. Describe Oliver's treatment of the natural world. What is the relationship between the speaker and the natural world?

3. Why does the speaker say, "remember"? To whom is the narrator speaking and what is to be remembered? How are these reminders related to the hawk?

Mary Oliver,
The Black Walnut Tree

1. Oliver writes "We talk/ slowly, two women trying in a difficult time to be wise." Why does she describe the women this way?

2. Why does the dream change the speaker's mind? What is the dream telling her?

3. What does the tree represent? Of what is it symbolic?

Mary Oliver,
Poem for My Father's Ghost

1. This poem is called "Poem for My Father's Ghost." What is the speaker saying to the ghost? Why might this poem address the father's ghost rather than the father?

2. At numerous times, Oliver repeats, "Now is my father." Why might this line be repeated? What is the effect of this repetition?

3. Explore the different images and settings that Oliver touches upon. Why does she include such a wide range of images and settings? What does this group of images and settings contribute to the poem?

Marge Piercy, Barbie Doll

1. What is Piercy saying about the social pressures on young girls? How is that message conveyed?
2. Why does Piercy call her poem "Barbie Doll"? What is implied through her allusion?
3. Compare stanzas 2 and 3. What does this comparison say about women and society's expectations of women?

Marge Piercy, A Work of Artifice

1. Consider the bonsai tree as the poem's central image. Is the tree a metaphor? If so, of what is it metaphoric?
2. Examine Piercy's poetic form. In particular, consider the line lengths. What effect is achieved through these line lengths? Is this effect significant to the poem and its subject matter?

Lucille Clifton, In the Inner City

1. In calling her poem "In the Inner City," Clifton sets up specific expectations. What expectations does she set up and what does she do with these expectations? Does she challenge or affirm them?
2. Clifton repeats four lines in this poem. What line gets repeated? Where is it repeated? Why do you think it is repeated?
3. Clifton contrasts "the inner city" with "uptown." What is revealed in this comparison and why do you think Clifton sets up this comparison?

Michael S. Harper,
Dear John, Dear Coltrane

1. Who is John Coltrane? How is Harper depicting Coltrane's life? What are the notable features of Harper's description of John Coltrane?

2. Read this poem out loud. What do you notice about the sound of this poem? Why is sound significant for this poem?

3. Describe Harper's use of italics. When, where, and why does he use them? What effect is achieved through Harper's use of italics?

Michael S. Harper,
Martin's Blues

1. The title of this poem alludes to Martin Luther King and the blues. How do both of these topics come together in this poem?

2. This poem is one of several in this anthology that alludes to King's story. How does this treatment of King compare with another writing that addresses King in this anthology?

3. Consider the poem's final four lines. What poetic strategies is Harper using? How are these lines significant to the rest of the poem?

Michael S. Harper,
"Bird Lives": Charles Parker in St.Louis

1. How is Harper using a written form to suggest a musical form? How is the poem suggestive of jazz and Charlie Parker?

2. How does Harper depict the life, context and significance of Charlie Parker? What is revealed about his music, life, and context and how is it revealed through poetic devices?

Paula Gunn Allen,
Pocahontas to her English Husband, John Rolfe

1. Who are Pocahontas and John Rolfe? What is the myth about them? How is Allen telling this story? What is notable about Allen's version of this story?
2. What is achieved through the use of the first person narrator? What is Allen able to do through this narrator? Why might she have chosen this particular narrator?
3. What kind of relationship is the character of Pocahontas describing? What is this relationship based upon? What is her tone toward Rolfe and to the life she led with him?

Gloria Anzaldúa,
To live in the Borderlands means you.

1. Examine the concept of the Borderlands. What are the Borderlands? What does it mean to live in a Borderland? How does one survive there?
2. Consider the way in which the Borderlands are described. How does Anzaldúa use poetic devices to convey and describe these borders?
3. Contrast, juxtaposition, and repetition are vital elements of this poem. Analyze Anzaldúa's use of these elements and describe what they contribute to the poem.

Joseph Bruchac III,
Ellis Island

1. Ellis Island plays a key role in the story of the twentieth century. Examine Bruchac's depiction of this place. How is he describing it? What is significant about his descriptions?
2. Philip Levine's poem, "The Mercy" is also about immigration to the U.S. and refers to Ellis Island. Combined, what issues do these poems raise about the immigrant experience?
3. Explore the significance of the line, "Yet only one part of my blood loves that memory." What does this line contribute to his discussion of Ellis Island and the Ellis Island mythology?

Sharon Olds, Rite of Passage

1. Why is the poem called "Rite of Passage"? How is this idea addressed in the poem?
2. Analyze Olds's use of imagery related to the boys. Can this poem be read as a commentary on gender?
3. Is the poem ironic or does it use irony? Why or why not?

Sharon Olds, The Victims

1. This poem is called "The Victims." To whom does this title refer? How are they victims? Is there more than one victim?
2. Olds uses the words "take" and "taken" frequently. Why is this an important word for this subject matter? What is taken and by whom?
3. In the first part of the poem, Olds refers to events in the past. In the second part, she refers to "now." Explain the significance of the past and present tense to the poem.

Tess Gallagher, The Hug

1. This poem describes a number of different relationships. Explain how this poem addresses relationships. What is it suggesting about the different kinds of relationships?
2. The title of this poem is "The Hug" yet there is more than one hug. Which hug do you think is "the hug"? Why?
3. What is suggested in the final sentence of the poem? How is this idea related to the previous lines in the poem?

Nikki Giovanni, Nikki-Rosa

1. Explain the role the biographers play. Why is she addressing them?
2. Examine Giovanni's use of the poetic form. Describe the style of this poem.

3. Describe the significance of the phrase "Black love is Black Wealth." How does Giovanni use this sentence? How is it illustrated in the poem?

Nikki Giovanni,
Master Charge Blues

1. As the editor notes, Giovanni uses language in "vivid, direct, expressive ways." Apply this comment to this poem. How is Giovanni using language in this poem?
2. Read this poem out loud. What do you notice about the sound of this poem? How would you describe it? How does Giovanni create this sound effect?
3. Why does the narrator call herself a "modern woman"? What makes the narrator think she's modern?

Louise Glück,
The Drowned Children

1. Consider this poem's tone. How would you describe this tone? How is the tone created? How is the tone related to the subject matter?
2. Examine Gluck's depiction of death. How is it described? What diction, imagery, and figurative language are used to describe death?
3. Do a close reading of the final stanza. How does it function as a conclusion to the poem? What is the function of the italics? What do they contribute to the poem?

Louise Glück,
Gretel in Darkness

1. Who is the narrator of the poem? What does the narrator reveal about herself and her past? What do we know about the narrator?
2. The title sets up several assumptions for the reader about the contents of this poem. Did this poem affirm or challenge your assumptions or expectations? How? Why?

3. What is revealed about Gretel's relationship with her brother? What is the state of that relationship? What are the factors that have influenced that relationship?

Louise Glück, Illuminations

1. In this poem, Glück creates three distinct sections. Why might she have created these sections? What is the effect of the sections and how are they related?
2. In each section, the narrator describes her son and the natural world. What is the relationship between the child and the natural world? How does each inform the other?
3. Language is mentioned in each stanza. How are words and language significant as a concept to this poem?

Louise Glück, Terminal Resemblance

1. Communication (or lack thereof) is an important element in this poem. How is communication addressed in this poem and why is it an important subject?
2. Among other things, this poem is about the relationship between the father and the narrator. What is the nature of this relationship and how is it conveyed through poetic strategies?
3. Examine the poem's title. What is suggested by "terminal resemblance"? What are the different ways in which this title can be read? How can these readings apply to the poem?

Yusef Komunyakaa, Facing It

1. The title has several levels to it. Examine the different meanings of "facing it" and describe how these different levels are conveyed in this poem.
2. Examine Komunyakaa's description of the Vietnam Veterans Memorial. How does he use this description for thematic purposes?

3. What do we know about the narrator? What can you tell about the impact of war from this speaker's point of view?

Joy Harjo, Call It Fear

1. Harjo repeats "There is this edge" at numerous points in the poem. What is "this edge" and why does this phrase recur in the poem?
2. Examine the physical layout of the poem. How is the poem placed on the page? What does the physical layout contribute to your understanding of the poem?
3. Explore Harjo's use of imagery. What ideas are conveyed by these images? How are the images related to the poem's larger themes and ideas?

Joy Harjo, White Bear

1. Harjo uses a number of images related to balance. Why is balance important to this poem? What is being balanced?
2. The flight forms a significant part of the poem. How is the flight used as a way into the concepts, images, and ideas raised in the poem?
3. Explain the function of the White Bear. What issues does Harjo explore through her? How does the bear work as an image?

Joy Harjo, Eagle Poem

1. Examine the imagery, diction, rhythm, and structure of this poem. How does Harjo attempt to pull all of these elements together for a particular effect? What is this effect? Why is this effect significant for this poem?
2. Explore Harjo's use of pronouns. Why are "you" and "we" important to this poem? Why might she have included them? How are "we" and "you" connected with the Eagle?

3. Prayer is mentioned at the beginning and end of this poem. Is this an important concept? How and why?

Jimmy Santiago Baca,
So Mexicans Are Taking Jobs From Americans

1. The editor cites Baca saying, "Poetry gives us the means to understand pain in a meaningless age. Language gives us insight into the darkness that we stumble into today." Examine this concept in relation to the poem.
2. Analyze the poem as a form of social commentary. What issues does this poem raise? This poem was first published in 1979. Is it still relevant today?
3. This poem offers a poignant look at socio-economic systems. What makes this a powerful poem? How is he using literary devices to create this poignancy?

Jimmy Santiago Baca,
Cloudy Day

1. Wind is a recurrent image in this poem. Where is wind used and how does it function as an image. What does it contribute to the poem?
2. Examine Baca's description of the prison. How is it described? How is Baca using literary devices to describe and comment upon the prison?
3. Do a close reading of the final stanza. What are the central elements of this stanza and how do these central elements function as a conclusion to the poem?

Rita Dove,
Daystar

1. The poem describes a woman's life. What does it suggest about women's lives? How is this woman's life described through poetic strategies?
2. Explain the significance of the title. What is the relationship between the title and the rest of the poem?

3. How is this poem about gender? What is it suggesting about gender and gender expectations. Compare this poem with another poem about gender in this anthology.

Rita Dove, Adolescence — I

1. The title of this poem establishes the topic of adolescence but the word is not mentioned in the poem. How is the topic of adolescence established in this poem?
2. Dove includes numerous sensory details. How are the senses evoked in this poem and why might Dove have wanted to evoke them? Why are senses important to this poem?
3. Linda and her words are placed in the center of the poem. Why has Dove placed Linda at the center of this poem? Why is she important?

Rita Dove, Adolescence — II

1. What is the subject matter of this poem? Support your answer with examples from the poem.
2. Who are the "three seal men"? What is their function in this poem?
3. What is the function of the darkness and nighttime imagery? Why is this imagery important to this particular poem?

Rita Dove, Straw Hat

1. Who is the "he" mentioned in the poem? What do we know about him, his past, his life, and his character? How is this information conveyed in the poem?
2. As the editor notes, Dove is "alert to the connections between personal and national histories." Can this statement be applied to this poem? How? Why?
3. When Dove writes, "He never knows when she'll be coming," who (or what) is the "she"? Why does he always tip his hat when she leaves?

Rita Dove,
Missing

1. Who is the narrator? What does Dove reveal about the "I"? Who is the "she" mentioned?
2. Explain the significance of the line "Now I understand she can never/ die, just as nothing can bring me back." How does this line relate to the poem as a whole?
3. Examine the final two lines of the poem. How are these two statements related to the poem as a whole and the ideas explored therein?

Judith Ortiz Cofer,
My Father in the Navy

1. Examine Cofer's diction. How is her father described and what is significant about her choice of words? What does this reveal about the narrator's thoughts about her father?
2. Analyze Cofer's use of figurative language. Where does she use it? How effective or evocative do you think her language is?
3. The narrator states her father was "an apparition on leave from a shadow-world." Why might Cofer have chosen this mode of describing the narrator's father?

Alberto Ríos,
Wet Camp

1. What is being described in this poem? How is the subject of the poem revealed?
2. Examine the first line of the poem? What work does it do in the poem? Do you find it to be an effective opening?
3. Look at Ríos's use of similes and metaphors. What do these contribute to the poem?

Alberto Ríos,
Advice to a First Cousin

1. Ríos states at the beginning, "The way the world works is this" and then halfway through states, "But the world works like this too." How are the two concepts related?
2. What is the difference between the two pieces of advice about scorpions? Is the advice only about scorpions or is it about something else as well? Why is the grandmother giving this advice?
3. Examine Ríos's choice of narrator and narrative structure. What does his choice of narrator and narrative structure allow him to do that would not have been possible through other narrative means?

David Mura,
An Argument: On 1942

1. The title makes reference to 1942. To what is the title alluding and why is the allusion important in order to understand the poem? How is 1942 addressed in the poem?
2. The title refers to an argument. What is the nature of this argument? The mother's side is heard; why has Mura left out the son's words in the argument? What do you assume to be the son's side? Even though Mura doesn't directly quote the son's part of the argument, do we still understand his point of view?
3. The mother says that the "camps are over . . . it was so long ago -- how useless it seems . . ." Do you think the mother believes these ideas? Does the son think his mother believes these things? Does he believe them?

Laureen Mar,
My Mother, Who Came from China, Where She Never Saw Snow

1. Examine Mar's depiction of setting. What is the setting? How is it described? Why is setting significant for this poem?

2. What is the narrator's tone toward the mother and her work? What is she suggesting about them both? What is the relationship between the mother and her work?

3. What is meant by the title? What does it add to the poem? Why is the mention of snow significant to the poem?

Lorna Dee Cervantes, Refugee Ship

1. Examine the structure of this poem. How are the three stanzas related? Different? What does this poetic structure and organization convey?

2. This poem mentions three generations. What is the relationship between the generations? How are the generations similar and/or different?

3. Explain the significance of the title and the line " I feel I am a captive/aboard the refugee ship."

Aurora Levins Morales, Child of the Americas

1. Examine Morales's description of the "I." How is the self depicted and defined? What is significant about this description?

2. Analyze Morales's use of figurative language and literary devices. What poetic strategies are used to describe the narrator and what is notable about Morales's use of language in this poem?

3. What is meant by the final two lines of the poem? How are these lines connected to the rest of the poem? Are these lines effective?

Cathy Song, The White Porch

1. This poem deals with time, memory, and reflection. Examine how memory is conveyed. What is the relationship between the memories and the present? How does Song reveal this relationship?

2. Who is the "you" in this poem? What is the narrator's relationship with this person?
3. Hair is mentioned numerous times. How does it function formally and/or thematically?

Cathy Song, Chinatown

1. Song uses highly sensory descriptions in this poem. Examine her use of imagery. Where is it most effective and what does the imagery contribute to your understanding of the poem?
2. This poem is divided into five sections. How does Song use the sections? Why might she have chosen to use sections and what is the relationship between the sections?
3. Family and family relationships recur in the poem. What is Song suggesting about this family and their relationships? How are these relationships connected to the Chinatown setting?

Cathy Song, Heaven

1. In this poem, Song juxtaposes places and generations. Examine the connections between places and generations.
2. Who is the "he" mentioned in the poem? How is "he" connected with heaven and with China?
3. Examine the significance of China to this poem. How and why is it significant?

Li-Young Lee, The Gift

1. Analyze how the narrator describes his father. What do we know of him? How is this information conveyed? What is the narrator's attitude toward the father?
2. Why does Lee use italics in the last two stanzas? What work do these italics do in the poem?
3. The poem is called "The Gift." What do you think the gift is?

Li-Young Lee,
Mnemonic

1. The poem's title alludes to memory and memory is a vital element in this poem as both an act and a concept. Examine the multiple ways memory is addressed in this poem.
2. Explore the significance of the blue sweater. How is it used in this poem and what function does it have?
3. What is the relationship between the son and the father? What does the son reveal about his relationship with his father? How is this relationship revealed through poetic devices?

Li-Young Lee,
This Room and Everything in It

1. Examine the form of this poem. What do you notice about Lee's use of form throughout the poem? What does the form contribute to your understanding of the poem?
2. Memory and love are important concepts to this poem. Examine Lee's treatment of these concepts.
3. Who is the "you" in the poem? What is the room? What is in it? How is the "you" connected with "This room and everything in it"?

Martin Espada,
Bully

1. Consider the references and allusions to Roosevelt. How is Espada using Roosevelt as an allusion and for what ends?
2. Espada uses the words "once" and "now." Examine how Espada uses past and present. What, according to this poem, is the relationship between past and present?
3. The poem is called "Bully." How is this concept related to the poem? Can this poem be read as a form of social commentary? If so, how?

Sherman Alexie,
On the Amtrak from Boston to New York City

1. Examine how the woman and the narrator differ in their responses to Walden Pond. Why and how do they approach it differently?
2. Describe Alexie's use of interior dialogue. What does it contribute to the poem? How is what he thinks different from what he says?
3. Analyze the concept of history. How is the narrator's view of history different from the woman's? Why is history important to both of them?